DAVID WILLIAMS is chairman of the Department of English, McGill University.

Cain, the inaugurator of social disharmony, bloodshed, and enmity among men, a commonplace of medieval exegetical tradition, is here examined by Dr Williams to illuminate the metaphoric use of the figure in the poem *Beowulf*.

The progenitor of the race of all monstrous creatures, Cain bequeaths to his descendants his own moral significance; thus Grendel and his mother, the giants, and all misbegotten creatures carry on the anti-social crusade he began with his fratricidal attack on Abel. In *Beowulf*, social dissension, personal bereavement, internecine destruction, the fall of nations, are the pre-eminent themes and are pre-eminently expressed through the figure of Cain: Cain explicit as the ancestor of Grendel and implicit as the spiritual father of all violent men. The fantastic and the historical, the temporal and the atemporal, are linked through the poem's peculiar allegorical use of Cain, himself both historical, scriptural, and a fantastic disfigurement in the legend of the monsters.

The *Beowulf* poet used the exegetical tradition to describe the anti-social force among men, forging, with biblical figures and moral truths, an allegory which is secular in the fullest medieval sense.

...lueurs ont senti et
...ir et mis en escript,
moult de choses de la
beneurte de paradis ou
de icellui paradis, et de la vie des pre-
miers hommes en icelli, et du pe-
chie et du tourment de iceulx, mais
nous auons dit es liures precedes
de ces choses selont les escriptures
saintes, ou ce que nous auons
leu en icelles, ou ce que nous auons
peu entendre dicelles en nous ac-
cordant a lautorite dicelles. Mar
le ces choses sont enquises plus
parfondement elles engendrent
tresplus orisons inanites et de main-
tes manieres, les queles sont
a estre compunies en plus de vo-
lumes, que ceste oeuure et le temps
ne requierent. Le quel temps nous

nauons mie si large que il nous
conuiengne de moustrer en toutes
les choses les queles ceulx peuent
demander qui sont oyseus et scau-
puleux et plus pres a demander
que il ne sont prenables a respon-
dre. Tout nous cuide ce que nous
auons ia asses fait, par que il les
grandes et tres fortes du commen-
cement du monde ou de lame
ou de icell humain lignage, le fil
nous auons deuise en .ij. maniee-
res. Cest assauoir tant de ceulx
qui viuent selonc homme. Et lautre de ceulx qui viuent selonc dieu. Les queles choses nous appel-
lons par vne maniere de secr-
rit mistere .ij. cites. Cest a dire .ij. co-
paignies de hommes. Des queles
lune est la quele est predestinee a
regner auecques dieu pardurablement.
Lautre est predestinee a recompenser et

DAVID WILLIAMS

Cain and Beowulf:
A Study in Secular Allegory

UNIVERSITY OF TORONTO PRESS
Toronto Buffalo London

© University of Toronto Press 1982
Toronto Buffalo London
Printed in Canada

ISBN 0-8020-5519-2

Canadian Cataloguing in Publication Data

Williams, David, 1939–
  Cain and Beowulf

  Bibliography
  Includes index.
  ISBN 0-8020-5519-2

  1. Beowulf.   2. Old English poetry – Criticism and
  interpretation.   3. Symbolism in literature.
  I. Title.

  PR1585.W54   8299.3   C81-094507-X

The illustration on page ii, showing Cain killing Abel, is from a manuscript of
St Augustine *De Civitate Dei*, Paris, Bibliothèque nationale, ms fr 22913, f 91v.

To the memory of
Elliot Williams and Anna Howard Williams

Acknowledgments

I would like to express my gratitude to the Humanities Grant Committee of the Faculty of Graduate Studies and Research of McGill University, whose generous support made the writing of this book possible. I wish to thank especially my colleagues, Professors Donald Bouchard, C. Abbott Conway, and Benjamin F. Weems, for reading the manuscript and making many substantial suggestions, and Valentina Matsangos, who prepared the typescript.

Publication of this book was made possible by a grant from the Canadian Federation for the Humanities, using funds provided by the Social Sciences and Humanities Research Council of Canada, and a grant from the Andrew W. Mellon Foundation to the University of Toronto Press.

DAVID WILLIAMS

Contents

CAIN AND BEOWULF:
A STUDY IN SECULAR ALLEGORY

1

Introduction

The present state of *Beowulf* scholarship would seem to indicate the general acceptance of the critical principle that medieval literature must be seen in its context of Latin-Christian intellectual traditions to be analysed and appreciated properly. It is, then, perhaps ironic that such wide acceptance of a critical principle has led to no greater degree of consensus on the meaning of *Beowulf* or its structure. It may be too hasty a conclusion that such lack of agreement demonstrates the failure of the principle itself, and we may need to look at its application.

The present discussion of *Beowulf* relies heavily on the Latin-Christian tradition behind the poem but not upon the theological expression of that tradition. Cultural context obviously includes not only the theological but also the general ethical, political, and aesthetic forms that are, properly speaking, secular even in the middle ages. Albeit in that period perhaps more than in others, theology often provides an interpretation for these forms. In this larger sense, then, it is argued here that *Beowulf* is very much a product of its time, a time of lingering ideological conflict and of the insecure triumph of the new social vision of Christianity.

Perhaps the best example of the difficulty encountered in viewing *Beowulf* as allegory is to be found in the seminal studies of Margaret Goldsmith and Charles Donahue.[1] Both Goldsmith and Donahue agree that the definitive influence on *Beowulf* and the poetic core of the poem are to be found in the Christian intellectual tradition, but disagreement is immediately apparent when each attempts to describe that tradition and its poetic expression. Donahue rightly objects that the allegorical analysis brought to bear upon the poem by Goldsmith leads her to a negative interpretation of the character of Beowulf difficult to sustain in light of the text and leads, as well, to a questionable interpretation of the church's attitude towards the pagan past. Equally right, Goldsmith objects to Donahue's application of typological interpretation as inappropriate to all but scriptural texts, and shows that his analysis identifies the poet's view of the past as one that seems to be contradictory to the presentation in the poem itself.

Goldsmith's excellent perception into the nature of the poem seems somewhat marred by what appears to be her effort, despite her own warning against it, to discover a consistent and technically perfect allegory in the theological sense. One can agree whole-heartedly with her sense of literary allegory in *Beowulf*: 'Allegory to these scholars [Bede, et al] was not a literary form, but, in the convenient phrase adopted by Angus Fletcher, "a symbolic mode" of thinking and writing. It is quite clear from the works I have just quoted that there was no theoretical separation of symbol and allegory; an allegorical work was simply one in which there was a great deal of hidden or obscure meaning conveyed in parable, enigma, proverb or almost any kind of metaphorical or ironic statement.'[2] But her pursuit of the allegorical theme, even one as general as 'man's struggle with sin,' seems to turn quickly into a description of a formal allegory of simple correspondences that accounts for her opting for the interpretation of the poem's pre-Christian hero as finally sinful and flawed. It is perhaps Goldsmith's desire to find this kind of allegorical correspondence and historical accuracy, rather than the poet's inability, that leads her to conclude: 'The potential of the ambitious design is not fully realized; the poet, brilliantly successful as he is at the great moments, does not always correlate his "historical" material and his many-faceted allegory.'[3]

If allegory can be taken as saying one thing to mean many things, or, as Angus Fletcher has described it, 'saying one thing in order to mean something beyond that one thing,'[4] we may be able to describe *Beowulf* generally as an allegory presenting historical reality that stands in analogy to other, non-historical realities. *Beowulf* as allegory says one thing about time as history and means many other things about time as transhistorical truth. The one meaning, of course, does not contradict the other, and indeed the two are complementary, but the historical 'accuracy' that might be found in a chronicle, or the allegorical formalness that might be dis-coverable in Scripture, cannot be expected here. *Beowulf*, it will be argued, is none the less an allegory, but a secular, literary allegory of a profound social vision.

The vehicle of that allegory is nevertheless of a very traditional kind and indeed of theological origin. The tradition of Cain, as developed from the earliest Christian exegesis on Genesis and reaching back for many of its features to pre-Christian formulations, was steadily transformed in the middle ages into legendary matter and is to be found in areas as far from scientific theology as literature, the visual arts, law, and history. While it may be admitted that the tradition of Cain as metaphor in the service of several cultural and intellectual structures is not contradictory to the original exegetical interpretation of Cain's significance, it is also noteworthy that as employed in medieval law the tradition is not necessarily subject to the same constraints as are faced by a theological writer. The use of the tradition is, however, whether in law or in literature, always highly didactic and ethical, and the ethical code is identical with that of theology, namely Christian ethics. Thus the distinction here is that while Christian theological science has informed the legend of Cain, its use by the *Beowulf* poet is not theological in the scientific sense, but a literary use of cultural legend deriving the same ethical lesson. Regardless of how we interpret the poet's attitude towards the pagan past, a problem essential to the poem's meaning, it is not necessary to discover, for instance, a liberal theologian of the eighth century as an authority for the poet's view.[5]

Therefore the present analysis of the allegorical quality of *Beowulf* emphasizes the historical and 'allegorical' dimensions over the other traditional levels of the tropological and anagogical. This emphasis itself reflects the view that in *Beowulf* we are dealing not with formal four-level allegory but with the more usual literary form of the two-level structure, history and allegory, or the literal and the symbolic. The analytical treatment of the tropological in this allegorical pattern is relatively light in comparison with the other 'levels' because its presence in the poem is seen as proportionately light. The present discussion is silent about the anagogical level because it seems that the poet is equally silent. The conclusion of this investigation is that the text itself cannot bear a fully developed, four-level reading, and the recent history of critical problems in *Beowulf* scholarship would seem to corroborate this view.

The perspective that is taken here is that *Beowulf* is a poem about the human-social condition bounded by the tropes of time as history and time as 'eschatophore.' It is in this sense that *Beowulf* is an allegory, but not like *The Divine Comedy*, which is a rare example of the theological system of allegory fully employed in the literary artifact. Rather, the allegory of *Beowulf* is in some ways more akin to that of *Troilus and Criseyde* in its metamorphosis of historical legend into metahistorical event.

The problems of the present study are to delineate the Cain tradition as it might have been available to the poet and thus to provide a source outside the poem that can be used to clarify the poetic intention and force of elements of the Cain tradition in *Beowulf*. I agree with Goldsmith (and several others) that the poem is likely a product of the eighth century,[6] but for the purposes of illustrating characteristics of the tradition that the poet uses, I make occasional reference to sources later than the likely date of composition of the poem. This is done on the theory that these late sources are the only textual references to characteristics of the tradition that are clearly much older than the existing reference. In addition to a general description of the nature and function of the Cain tradition in the early middle ages, I cite here only those texts that seem to have bearing on the poet's use of the tradition in *Beowulf*.

The second problem is encountered in reconstructing the general social context into which the use of the Cain tradition as seen in *Beowulf* is to be fitted. Since any such reconstruction will necessarily be partial, I have tried to be guided by the apparent themes of the poem. *Beowulf* makes frequent allusion to kinship, loyalty, peace, war, betrayal, and hatred, among other references. It does not give an important place to commerce, technology, or sexual mores, for instance, and so in the passing comments on the cultural and social forms prevalent at the time of the composition of the poem those phenomena that are alluded to in *Beowulf* are emphasized. This reconstruction is necessary if we can assume – and there is much evidence that would allow us to – that *Beowulf*, while situated in various moments of the poet's and audience's past, is not simply an antiquarian poem but speaks to social and philosophical concerns of its contemporary audience through analogy to the past.

A salient feature of early Anglo-Saxon society was the structural importance of the kin, and kinship is at heart a tribal concept the chief function of which is the protection of its members. Those outside the kin are seen socially, ethically, and sometimes legally as 'other' – not encompassed by the rights and protections of those who belong. The primary moral values of such a concept are fidelity to one's fellow member and the avenging of wrongs done to him. Vengeance, then, takes on the aspect of sacred obligation since it is the ultimate assurance of protection of the group, and one readily perceives this value expressed in the literature of the time.

In Anglo-Saxon history, as well, we perceive the frequency of feud since this is the inevitable outcome of the practice of vengeance between clans strong enough to fulfil continually their obligation to avenge a loss. Since there is, in fact, little attention paid to right and wrong in such a system, but rather primacy given to the questions of loss and restitution, any clan that loses a member through the avenging of that member's assault upon another will feel the right and obligation to avenge him in turn. Thus the feud:

The most primitive idea as to the nation is that it is a kindred, enlarged past all remembered degrees of relationship, but holding to a tradition of common ancestry, human or divine ... This sense of common blood is carried deeply into the structure of the nation. The rank, status, and privilege of each man are his birthright. They are only valid if he can establish their inheritance from four generations and point to a full kindred extending through four degrees of descent ... Early law cannot and will not deal with the individual. The actions of every man involve his kinsmen, and they share his responsibility. The most striking instance of this is the feud. In slaying or injuring another the offender not only brings upon himself the enmity of his victim's kin, but involves his own. By the act of the individual the families of both parties – to seven or nine degrees according to usage – are legally open to vengeance or committed to taking it, though they may, if they like, pay the heavy blood-price or *wergeld* to 'buy off the spear.'[7]

To the Christian missionary the system must have seemed barbaric indeed. Not only did the Christians consider the ethic of vengeance to be spiritually limiting and demeaning, but further, in assessing its catastrophic effects, such as feud, on the peace and good functioning of society, they found in the pagan concepts of tribal exclusivity and blood vengeance the major obstacles to their ideological mission.[8]

The social-calamity potential in feud is obvious, and much of Anglo-Saxon history attests to its realization. Without any Christian encouragement the pagan Germans sought ways of mitigating its effects, and thus we see the development of the wergeld system. Wergeld was essentially a method of restitution in which a scale of monetary values was placed on various members of society so that their death or injury could be appropriately compensated. The philosophical emphasis in wergeld is not on the guilt or innocence of the perpetrator of a crime but on the concrete effect of the act itself. It is conceptually a near relative of the idea of 'an eye for an eye,' which makes no place for a sense of circumstances, intent, or wrong. Moreover, it underscores the central, exclusive importance of the kin to which the wergeld must be paid. Because all offences are seen from the point of view of the unity and its loss, and not from that of the offended individual, the fact that a freeman pays less for the killing of a churl than for the killing of another freeman is not perceived as unjust. Every clan is made up of freemen and churls and others, and whatever is lost is what must be repaid.

The Christians found in the wergeld system something they could employ for their own purposes, and it was continued by them to prevent widespread feud. But to this system they added the revolutionary concept of sin. With this distinction we notice one important difference between pagan and Christian law: the latter is as concerned with the disposition of the criminal as with the compensation of the victim. Thus in the seventh-century penitential of Theodore we note the attempt to assess the motive of the accused in assigning punishment for homicide: 'He who has killed a man in anger shall do penance for three years. If the crime occurs by accident, one year; if by poison or by craft, four years or more; and if the murder takes place as part of a quarrel, ten years.'[9]

With the slow evolution of the idea of sin comes the sense of personal guilt and innocence, the possibility of accidental commission of crime, and the importance of intention – all of which tend to diminish the exclusivity of the criterion of the effect of the act and to promote an awareness of the individual and of the state: 'In Anglo-Saxon as well as other Germanic laws we find that the idea of wrong to a person or his kindred is still primary, and that of offence to the common weal secondary, even in the gravest cases. Only by degrees did modern principles prevail that the members of the community must be content with the remedies afforded them by law, and must not seek private vengeance ...'[10]

In addition to the adoption and expansion of the wergeld system as a legal instrument in the Christianization of Britain, the missionaries and native converts attempted to transform or weaken the social system of tribal fidelity by the promotion of central government personified by the king. A single strong ruler to replace the numerous war-lords and petty princes favoured the Christian missionaries' goals, not only for immediate, pragmatic reasons but also by encouraging the development of long-term attitudes more conducive to their ideology. The very existence of small political units bespoke their philosophical basis in the exclusive mentality of blood ties. The emergence of the notion of the state, on the other hand, freed citizens from this confining moral relationship by adding to it the further relation of individual to national society, a family of men interrelated by common political and moral values. Subtle reinforcements of the idea are met with repeatedly in the history of Anglo-Saxon Christianity.

In and of itself the concept of the king's peace is perhaps a small step, but it was an important one in the changing mentality, for it asserts, even if indirectly, that the king and the state are a party to all breaches of the law, that the king may punish and remain exempt from vengeance, and that in general society has a stake in how its members behave. As this concept develops and is reinforced, a larger and larger share of the stake is claimed for the state, until – only after centuries, to be sure – the mind of the Englishman accepts as a moral principle that in any crime the greatest offence is against the law itself. At such a point society has transcended its tribal phase. Part of this evolution can be seen in the changes over the years of the period we are here discussing in, for instance, the assignment and division of the payments of fines. We see the introduction of the idea that not only should the offended kin receive wergeld, but a small portion should be awarded, as well, to the king whose law has been broken. A larger and larger portion of this wergeld is legislated away from the offended kin to the offended king as Christian lawmakers work away at their task.

Of particular importance in the evolution of modern social structures and the replacement of kinship bonds is the peculiar problem posed by the crime of parricide, by which is meant the killing of a member of one's family. Because loss and restitution are seen as concerning the clan only, an ethical dilemma of major proportion occurs with the murder of one kinsman by another. The surviving kinsmen can neither exact vengeance on the killer, since even his death must be avenged, nor seek compensation, since in so doing they would fine themselves. Parricide, to a degree far greater than any other crime, shook pagan social structures to the roots.

Christianity held the crime in no less horror, but for different reasons. Murder of one's kin, which scripturally was the way in which death entered the world, was looked upon as the most complete negation of the Christian vision of the charitable social existence of all men as God's children. But because of the Christian emphasis on the spiritual state of the offender as well as the idea of sin as primarily an offence against God, chastisement of the parricide was possible. The penitentials of the Christian middle ages are replete with punishments for the parricide that are nuanced according to intention and the circumstances surrounding the crime. The gravity of the act is attested to by the fact that parricide is regularly punished by double the time of fasting and exile as is homicide. Thus the penitenitals develop a means of atonement for this crime that pagan justice cannot resolve by emphasizing the nature of the offence as one against God, the self, and the state.

This social context is by and large that of the early Christian society transforming its heathen institutions into Christian ones. The resistance of the pagan institution of kinship to this transformation is a central theme both of Anglo-Saxon history and of *Beowulf*. With its reliance on the ethical and legal efficacy of vengeance and feud, the pagan institution of exclusive kinship was irreconcilable with the Christian vision of universal kinship or brotherhood. So basic was it, however, to the social and psychological structures of the Anglo-Saxons, and for that matter of all Europeans, that the ethic of vengeance was eliminated as a social value only after centuries of patient undermining by Christian propagandists. The historical moment of the composition of *Beowulf* is one in which the success of the Christian mission to universalize the concept of kinship and eliminate vengeance as an ethic could not have been predicted with sureness. The presentation by the *Beowulf* poet of a panorama of the social and moral disasters of the past resulting from this ethic suggest not only that the poem is one of social relevance to its immediate audience, but that its function is didactic and ideological. The vehicle of this presentation is the legend of Cain.

The tradition of the descent of the monsters from Cain has particular importance to *Beowulf*, as much recent critical consideration indicates,[11] yet certain facets of the tradition, particularly its cultural-historic character and its allgeorical dimension, remain less than fully described. The application of these aspects of the tradition to the *Beowulf* allusions is also incomplete.

While the present study does not attempt to identify the author of *Beowulf*, it is nevertheless necessary because of other claims to suggest something about the kind of person who could have written such a poem and to describe, however briefly, the cultural and intellectual climate that would have made possible the writing of the kind of poem that *Beowulf* is here seen to be. Whatever the historic reality of the Anglo-Saxon scop, whether as literary metaphor or historical figure, his description in Old English is consistent and informative. Lewis F. Anderson long ago perceived his social role as one transcending casual entertainment: 'It is possible that the scop was looked upon as one whose function was not merely to entertain but also to instruct. The sagas that he repeated to the old Germans were to them something far different than what they are to us. They embodied their history and their theology.'[12]

The author of *Beowulf*, whether or not a scop in the strict sense, is seen in the present discussion as a man who combined native cultural memorialization of a Germanic past with Christian propaganda towards the realization of a social vision of Christian justice. Such an author possessed at least the normal acquaintance with patristic commentary and historical theory of an educated cleric of the time and a familiarity with native poetry and tradition. We may well assume that every poet is unique and capable of intellectual innovations, but would an audience of eight- or ninth-century Britain have greeted sympathetically such a possibly daring combination of exegesis and native poetry?

It is not at all impossible that at a moment such as the one we are describing we find ourselves at the beginning of some sort of national revival in Britain; not one, to be sure, antagonistic to Latin culture and intellectual heritage, but one that revalorizes the native traditions and attempts to synthesize them with the new classical heritage. It may be legitimate, if speculative, to see in Bede's discussion of the loss of Latin an indication of the revival of Anglo-Saxon among the educated.[13] Whatever the case may be, the Anglo-Saxon poet was by social necessity and tradition a historian since the events of the past, as legend or as fact, were properly his subject matter, and even in his purely Germanic, pagan past he was associated with the true and the holy: 'First, the singer was not only a man distinguished by his skill in almost the only fine art which the Anglo-Saxon cultivated, but he was the curator of their literature and of their religious and historical myths, and something of the religious character of the primitive poetry adhered to the professional singer.'[14] As Anderson also points out, the Christian Anglo-Saxon continued to identify the poet with the holy man, and he calls attention to Cynewulf's description of Moses as a singer.[15] Conceptually the combination of cleric-scop would seem to have been easy for such a society, but is there any evidence that such a combination was embodied in a living figure?

The history of the period offers innumerable examples of educated clerics, men with great familiarity with Christian writing who were also associated with Anglo-Saxon courts and thus dedicated to the native political and historical interests of those courts. King Peada of the Middle Angles as early as the seventh century had four priests attached to him, while in Mercia Wulfhere also had priests at court. Bishop Agilbert had served King Coinwalch of Wessex at about the same time, and later King Alfred, too, surrounded himself with clerical advisers. Benedict Biscop was a member of King Oswy's comitatus. As Clinton Albertson has pointed out in his discussion of the Germanic, heroic style of such Anglo-Saxon poetry as *Elene*, *Andreas*, *Guthlac*, and *Dream of the Rood*, the authors of these works were educated monks who had joined the monasteries after a youthful education in an aristocratic Saxon family. Steeped in Germanic themes and tradition, these young Anglo-Saxon Christians later underwent a classical Christian education. But they did not forget their own heritage. What is more likely than that the clerical student of the seven liberal arts would employ the scriptural knowledge he had, as well as his newly found rhetorical skills, to fulfil the beauty and truth that clearly lay in his native themes? As Albertson says: 'Seeing *Beowulf* in the context of an Anglo-Saxon monastery should be no puzzle at all. Anglo-Saxon Christian poems like *Andreas* and *Elene* and *Guthlac*, cast in the mold of the old heroic poetry, seem quite in place, and so do the diction and alliteration from heroic poetry that seem almost by force of habit to have made their way into monastic Anglo-Saxon prose translations of Latin Lives, like that of St. Chad.'[16]

Doubtless the best example of the combination of Latin, ecclesiastical scholarship, and native political activity is found in Alcuin of York, who acted essentially as Charlemagne's minister of education and culture. Alcuin's own aesthetic endeavours, however, were in Latin, not in the vernacular. In this sense the model of the cleric possessing familiarity with patristic texts and knowledge and skill in native poetry is better filled by a figure of the late seventh, early eighth century who synthesized Latin learning and Germanic traditions to a degree no other known to us did. William of Malmesbury describes the coming together of intellectual text and bardic art, scholarship and rhetoric, when he depicts St Aldhelm's practice of forming a bridge, as it were, between history and legend by clothing his didactic lesson in the cloak of native poetry: 'This blessed man would stand upon a bridge spanning city and country, like a poet. He recited tales into which he would weave words of Scripture with more secular themes. Thus he lead the people to holiness.'[17]

Were men like Aldhelm so rare? In degree of accomplishment, perhaps, but in his origins, training, and mentality Aldhelm may be taken as rather typical of the well-educated, civilized man of his time. William tells us that he sprang from a noble Saxon family and was educated by the Abbot Adrian, learning Greek and Latin. In later life he became a teacher and was famous for his intellectual achievements. Still later he returned, as William tells us, 'to the feet of Adrian, who was the font of literary learning.'[18] Despite his extraordinary accomplishments in the Greek and Latin liberal arts, or perhaps because of them, Aldhelm placed great value on the poetry of his native Old English, and, we may assume, in addition to composing in that language, was familiar with other writings in it.[19] William tells us as much: 'So, fully instructed in literature, he did not neglect the songs of his native tongue. So much so that, witness the book of Eldfred, mentioned above, he was unequaled in any age. He could write English poetry, compose songs, and recite them or sing them, as was most fitting.'[20]

Aldhelm, exposed not only to the Irish spiritual and intellectual tradition of Maelduib but also the Greco-Latin humanism of Theodore of Tarsus and Hadrian, was in an excellent position as a native Saxon for synthesizing such strains in the English context. The school of Theodore in the mid-seventh century augmented ecclesiastical teaching with secular learning, and it is likely that with this renaissance of intellectual vigour in Britain the value of purely secular, or 'pagan,' wisdom increased considerably.

Aldhelm, as well as other students at Canterbury, studied Latin and Greek in order to gain direct access to the writings of the Fathers; emphasis on exegetical commentary, allegorical interpretation, and moral theology characterized this new school, and it may be ventured that no text more than *The City of God*, as well as Augustine's other works, would have been subject of study there, considering Hadrian's enthusiasm for the author.[21] From such an education the Saxon student gained entry into the intellectual universe beyond his native land: the encyclopaedic writings of such an author as Isidore, an important name in the liberal-arts education of the time; the historical and polemical work of such a writer as Orosius; and the legal theory and tradition of the Roman Empire.

From William of Malmesbury's words and those of Faricio describing St Aldhelm we derive a portrait of a man and of an intellectual climate in which native tradition and classical learning were perceived as complementary and integratable rather than contradictory. A man of Aldhelm's learning did not choose to compose poetry in the language and style of the Germanic tradition if he and his audience considered that tradition trivial or misleading; more likely, he did so because in the new learning were discovered the tools needed to bring forth from that native literature the buried truth, as well as the means to relate that truth to the universal social vision of Christianity.

Such a climate is one in which a poem like *Beowulf* is likely to have been written, if the present reading of the poem is at all valid. The author of such a poem would need to have been a man not unlike Aldhelm, steeped in Latin and Christian learning and imbued with a love of native form. I doubt if such men were as rare as has sometimes been suggested. As William Whallon has perceptively pointed out: '*Beowulf*, because of its being written in West Saxon, seems likely to have been washed in the currents he [Aldhelm] created.'[22] And indeed those currents would seem to have been wide and long-flowing enough to have produced a generation of men among whom one possessed, in addition to an ideological concept based on Christian intellectual training and a love of his native traditions, the spark of poetic genius.

This is an important background to the present discussion of the poem since in the more detailed analysis of the text that follows no effort is made to give equal weight to those passages of *Beowulf* that may be seen to portray the more positive aspects of heroic society. The ultimate vision of the poet is a tragic one, but it is not anti-heroic or anti-pagan. The tragedy is much larger than that. The poem is filled with good and great figures of the pagan past, and Beowulf, without being a Christ figure, is the greatest of them. But the present reading of the poem attempts to show why these figures are ultimately defeated and how, in the poem's dialectic of time, they are replaced and the struggle goes on. The poetic vehicle for this statement is the Cain tradition as explicated here, and while that tradition implies the character of Abel and a whole series of prefigurations of the good, its emphasis is on Cain and his historic and symbolic significance. Just as Beowulf is not a Christ figure, he is not an Abel figure, either, for we are not involved with formal typology in this poem. Similarly, while the *Beowulf* poet repeatedly describes the goodness and glory of the heroic, pagan past, his emphasis is on its collapse, and that emphasis is achieved through the use of the Cain metaphor. In the present analysis of how the poet employs this metaphor to create the poem's dialectic of time, my emphasis, as well, has been on those parts of the poem that illuminate this dimension.

The second chapter of the present study attempts to establish the characteristics of the Cain tradition through an examination of texts of exegetical, legal, and social character ranging from the earliest biblical commentaries to a few texts dating as late as the tenth century. Because of their special influence on medieval thought in general as well as the fullness of their writings on the Cain story, Ambrose, Augustine, Jerome, and Bede are emphasized.

The occasional use of Hebrew commentary and legend does not imply an assumption that the Anglo-Saxons had access to Hebrew texts or the ability to read them, since the little evidence that exists indicates the opposite. Nevertheless, many of the features of Christian exegesis and medieval legend have their origin in Hebrew tradition, although the history of their transmission is complex and incomplete. The chief means of transmission of such material was the Latin commentary of the early Christian writers who read Hebrew, like Jerome, or who had otherwise gained access to this legend. Of particular importance to the Cain tradition are Philo and Josephus, both obviously able to transmit Jewish beliefs and widely read by Christian commentators. Josephus' influence on Bede, for instance, was considerable, and Bede's use of him as a source, particularly in the *Ecclesiastical History*, demonstrates one route of transmission of Jewish legend into Anglo-Saxon. In Bede's case, indeed, Plummer has suggested[23] in a particular instance that Bede must have had direct or indirect knowledge of Talmudic legend when he composed his lines on the giants in Genesis 2: 'They speak of that which was the greatest provocation of the giants, that they ate meat mixed with blood; therefore, the Lord, having obliterated them in the Flood, conceded to man that he might eat meat, but He forbade that he mix it with blood.'[24] There is some indication that St Aldhelm, too, knew Hebrew as well as Latin and Greek and had access to writings in that language: 'St Aldhelm knew well the exempla of the Prophets, David's psalms, the three books of Soloman, as well as Hebrew literature and the Mosaic laws.'[25]

As we shall see, Bede's description of the giants is typical in the medieval tradition of Cain and is reflected in the poetic discussion of history in *Beowulf*. If Bede and others did have direct access to Talmudic legend, there is no evidence now to corroborate it.[26] What is significant, however, is his awareness of the substance of the Jewish legend that linked the Cain-descended monsters to blood taboos that were extended in both Hebrew and Christian commentary to include cannibalism.

One of the Hebrew legends referred to below is that of Cain's cohabiting with his mother, Eve. This tradition was widely known in Anglo-Saxon England, not necessarily through familiarity with the Jewish original but through knowledge of Christian exegesis. No less a figure than Augustine becomes a vehicle when he refutes the idea in a passage in *On Nature and Grace*: 'Scripture has indeed omitted to mention concerning the few persons who were then in existence, either how many or who they were–in other words, how many sons and daughters Adam and Eve begat, and what names they gave them; and from this circumstance some, not considering how many things are quietly passed over in Scripture, have gone so far as to suppose that Cain cohabited with his mother.'[27]

Nor was Augustine the only such source. The established legend of Jewish lore that Cain was originally sired by Satan is strongly echoed in Scripture itself when it is said: 'Not as Cain who was of the wicked one' (1 John 3:12) Tertullian provides an allegorical version of the idea, further disseminating the theme of Cain's diabolical parentage: 'Having been conceived of the seed of the Devil, she [Eve] immediately through the fecundity of evil gave birth to Anger, her son.'[28] St John Chrysostom allegorized the idea into the figure of Cain's vices as the children of the Devil,[29] and later exegesis continued to allegorize the original Hebrew idea, illustrating at once its structural importance to the Cain legend and, we may say, its general prevalence in medieval thought. Rupertus, the German abbot of the twelfth century, explains as allegorical the designation of Cain as Satan's offspring in John: 'First Cain sprang from the seed of the Devil. Thus John in his epistle: "Not as Cain," he said, "who was of the evil one." He was therefore of the seed of the serpent, not biologically, but in the sense of his imitation of evil.'[30] This 'seed of the Devil,' Rupertus further explains, spreads itself quickly over the earth, and he includes in the offspring of Satan the daughters of men of Genesis 6, an idea of Hebrew origin.

The use of Hebrew legend in the present study is solely for the purpose of filling out the details of the Cain tradition as it might have been known in the middle ages. The history of transmissions of such lore is not directly pertinent to the argument brought forth herein, which rests rather on the nature of the Cain tradition in the early middle ages and the appearance of aspects of that tradition in the poem *Beowulf*. Naturally, however, the pertinence of any of the details of this tradition rests upon the possibility of its having been known to the Anglo-Saxon community of the author of *Beowulf*. In 'Cain's Monstrous Progeny in *Beowulf*,' a thorough study of the Noachic elements of the Cain legend, Ruth Mellinkoff very convincingly demonstrates the availability of the Hebrew legends to the *Beowulf* poet and presents persuasive arguments that the poet consciously employed materials from the Book of Enoch in his use of the Cain legend:

My suggestion is, therefore, that the *Beowulf* poet did not merely tack on to Grendel and his mother derivation from Cain as a piece of literary embellishment but that probably he owed several formative concepts in his portrayal of these monsters to ancient Noachic tradition. That he should have been in a position to do so need not surprise us. For one thing there is nothing inherently unlikely in the general supposition that Jewish lore, both the ancient pre-rabbinic kind contained in the pseudepigrapha such as the ancient Noah story, and the later classic rabbinic ideas in Talmud and Midrash (which themselves were influenced by the ancient pseudepigrapha), was known in Anglo-Saxon England at the time of the composition of *Beowulf*.

In most cases we must be satisfied with the demonstration that a given commentary or legend could have been known, for rarely can we assert in Anglo-Saxon literary criticism that a given text was definitely known by a given poet whose own identity is often unknown. The final test of such pertinence for a literary critic probably remains whether or not a given parallel helps to elucidate the poetic text. An example of this might be the description of Grendel drinking the blood of his victims. In the chapter on the tradition of Cain the reader is referred to the story in the Book of Adam and Eve in which Cain drinks Abel's blood after the murder. To my knowledge there is no solid historical evidence that this pseudepigrapha was known to the Anglo-Saxons, despite its wide popularity in the middle ages generally. There is, however, some evidence that the ideas of the Book of Enoch were transmitted through Tertullian, Clement of Alexandria, and Athenagoras, and such ideas include the blood drinking and cannibalism of Cain's progeny.

The few citations of Jewish legend in the present study are usually subjects of indirect transmission. To any Anglo-Saxon familiar with Scripture and the standard exegesis of Jerome, Augustine, Gregory, Ambrose, Philo, and Josephus, the themes contained in these citations were readily available.

In the third chapter an attempt is made to examine *Beowulf* in light of this tradition; the significance of Grendel as a descendent of Cain and Beowulf's opposition to him are discussed as the fundamental metaphor of the poem. The traditional allegorization of Cain as every violent and antisocial force and the theme of his demonic parentage are seen here as the metaphoric connection between Beowulf's battle with Grendel and his fight with the dragon.

An examination of the 'digressions' in chapter four from the the point of view of the allegory of the Cain figure in history attempts to demonstrate that, as opposed to digressions in the strict sense, these incidents are part of the full allegorical pattern extending temporally forward and backward the theme established in the poem's 'present'; that is, the so-called main themes of Beowulf and Grendel, Beowulf and the dragon.

The last chapter refers to these elements of historical perspective and metaphoric use of Cain and attempts to describe the particular quality of allegory that exists in *Beowulf*. A brief discussion of the social values at play in the poem and in the poet's society concludes by trying to illustrate the relationship between the poem's allegorical substance and its didactic social intent.

This examination of *Beowulf* adopts the view that the poem presents a complex vision of history and society focusing on the struggle of societies to evolve institutions and moral codes that will ensure the survival of civilization. The mode of presentation of this theme is the allegorization of history and legend in which the struggles of an essentially fabulous nature of a hero against the monsters are intertwined with historical event and become its paradigm. The nature of Beowulf, like that of Cain, his ultimate antagonist and the progenitor of the monstrous race, is simultaneously historical and fabulous. While we can see the hero participate in the temporal and geographic incidents of the poem as a young retainer proving his mettle and later as political ruler, it would seem that the poet has deliberately left imprecise much in his historical portrait. Beowulf's genealogy – his mother nameless, his father a shadowy figure – is less clear than that of other characters. We do not see him, as we do other major characters, in his domestic life with wife and child. He has no heir. Even his name tends to dissociate him from maternal and paternal lineage. His primary function in the poem is in his opposition to the monsters, and he emerges as the figure who represents the ethical principles contradicted in the ravages of these monsters: brotherhood, loyalty, peace keeping, and lawful government.

In this sense it is difficult to see the poem as one depicting the hero's personal struggle with sin. The commonplace that medieval poets, unlike modern writers, did not explore individual human psychology or develop character has perhaps been overstated, but even the universalized form of personal moral dilemma to be found, for example, in *The Seafarer*, is not to be found in the portrait of Beowulf, although the descriptions of such characters as Wealhtheow and Hrethel attest to the poet's ability to depict tragedy. Beowulf does not struggle with sin any more than Grendel struggles with virtue, but provides instead the measure of the virtue attained in past civilization by which historical figures can be judged and their societies understood.

Beyond this civilization stands the Christian vision of ideal society formed by metaphysical, historical, and moral principles referred to regularly in the poem and providing the ideological basis for the understanding of what the poem presents. Thus, while Beowulf represents the highest standards of virtue in the poem, he does not represent the ideal Christian ruler nor does his realm symbolize the ideal Christian society, ultimately unattainable on earth. He is neither a Christian nor a Christ figure nor an Old Testament type, for the allegory of the poem does not seem to work in that way. He is poetically conceived as quite like his contrary, for as Grendel is simultaneously the historical descendant and spiritual representative of Cain, Beowulf is metaphorically one of the 'sons of God,' symbolically representative of the moral goodness of man that moves, however inconsistently and in whatever time, towards the Christian ideal of social harmony and civilized order.

The tragic reversals in this movement found their explanations in Christian thought through the allegorical description of Cain and the continuity of his force through a race of monsters. The didactic purpose of *Beowulf* is achieved through the application of this allegory to levels of historic time presented in the poem as past, present, and future in the various spatial loci of Denmark, Finnsburg, Sweden, and Geatland.

2

The Cain Tradition

The principal scriptural renditions of the Cain and Abel story are found in the Septuagint and the Vulgate, and each possesses important differences from the other that influenced certain features of later exegesis. The Septuagint described Cain's curse as groaning and trembling (Genesis 4: 12–13), while the Vulgate described it as his being an exile and outcast. The Septuagint spoke of his going out to dwell in Nod; the Vulgate describes his dwelling as 'east of Eden' (Genesis 4:15). Most significantly, the Septuagint in describing the first population of earth and the rise of the giants relates the intercourse of the 'sons of God' with the 'daughters of men,' making the giants the progeny of this union. Indeed, the Alexandrian manuscript of the Septuagint gives 'angels of God' in the place of 'sons of God,' forming the basis of later interpretation that these 'giants' were the result of sexual intercourse between spiritual beings and human women and thus of mixed, or 'monstrous,' nature. The Vulgate, on the other hand, refers only to the 'sons of God' and merely reports the existence of giants on earth without specifying their parentage (Genesis 6:1–4).

The biblical commentators knew both versions of the story and frequently combined elements from each of them in their interpretations. Thus in exegesis Cain is said to be cursed both 'trembling and groaning' and as 'wanderer and exile.' One of the most confusing discrepancies was that between the identification of the 'sons of God' in the Vulgate and, in the Alexandrian version of the Septuagint, the 'angels of God.' One finds both versions adopted in commentary, but later exegetes generally favoured the Vulgate reading, interpreting 'sons' as the righteous line of Seth. However, the influence of the other reading, providing as it did the basis for all magical and monstrous characteristics of the Cain tradition, made itself felt throughout commentary and was essentially uneradicable.

Despite the fact that the Bible is quite clear concerning the pedigree of the first man born on earth, exegetical speculation beginning in rabbinical lore and continuing through late medieval commentary posited alternative genealogies. Hebrew commentary seeking an explanation of Cain's extraordinary depravity attributed to him extraordinary and depraved parentage through the theory of cohabitation between Eve and the Devil.[1] Here we discover an echo of the medieval tradition that all monsters are descended from Cain and that both Cain and his descendants were marked by a fantastic appearance, the details of which varied from time to time and place to place as the exegetical tradition borrowed from local cultural traditions of monsters and spirits. Originally in Judaeo-Christian culture the monster was a creature of mixed natures, angelic and human, from which he derived peculiar strength of body and mind.

Thus in Hebrew and Christian commentary Cain and his descendants as the progeny of Satan were seen as Satan's tools in his on-going efforts to destroy man. Early Christian exegesis stated Cain's relationship to the Devil in literal terms; later commentators stated the same relationship as allegorical, but the idea of Cain as Devil-related was never contradicted, just as the similar idea of angels cohabiting with women survived in one form or the other. Goldsmith's assertion that 'the poet has no truck with rabbinical legends that the Devil fathered Cain upon Eve'[2] seems somewhat too absolute. While one would hardly wish to assert that the *Beowulf* poet had direct knowledge of Hebrew legends, the monstrous description of Grendel in the poem allows us to suppose that he was influenced by later commentary and tradition that had previously been influenced by rabbinical lore.[3]

Thus through allegorical understanding the Hebrew idea that Cain was sired by Satan found its way into Christian exegesis in more acceptable form. As this aspect of the tradition developed into the late middle ages, Cain was seen as the tropological figure of the Devil, his son through moral imitation, not natural lineage. This moral relationship between the force of evil in the world and Cain became the basis of the allegorical significance of history, since Cain founded a race of men who lived in spiritual imitation of the father and who were to be found everywhere on earth. They are and always will be true to their origins in envy and murder, and they build cities and states to satisfy their lust for power.[4]

Generally Cain is associated with his mother, Abel with his father. Thus the important distinction in their professions is given a rationale. The Anglo-Saxon poem *Genesis* reflects this part of the tradition:

Oðer his to eorðan   elnes tilode,
se wæs ærboren;   oðer æhte heold
fæder on fultum. (972–4)

The strong association of Cain with the animal was bolstered by the
etymology of his name, features of his birth and profession, and his
irrational existence in Nod. Allegorically the association with the animal
permitted the use of Cain as a figure for animal appetite,[5] often specified as
blood-lust, and further as a figure for the synagogue as opposed to the
Church.[6] His status as first-born corroborated his association with
animality since it was a principle of Christian allegory that the animal
precedes the spiritual (see 1 Corinthians 15:46). St Augustine built the
entire metaphor of the two cities on this principle, assigning Cain and Abel
as their representatives and thus giving the fundamental trope to the
Christian philosophy of history. The moral-literal expressions of this
association of Cain with the animal, however, were responsible for the
important features of the tradition by which animals came to be seen
increasingly as the most appropriate representation of monsters. Ideas
such as cannibalism, bestiality, and demon worship were introduced to the
portrait of Cain's descendants in connection with this animal quality.[7] The
medieval commentator apparently saw no contradiction between Cain's
bestiality and his profession as tiller of earth, rather than shepherd. Indeed,
allegorically the two features are seen as complementary, for the 'animal
soul' is described as 'earth-bound,' and cupidity as love of earthly things is
regularly identified as the animal side of man and signified by the beast.
Abel's husbandry, on the other hand, was seen as a prefiguration of the
Good Shepherd theme,[8] the protection of the flock of domesticated animals
from the savagery represented by the untamed beast.

Although orthodox exegesis saw in Cain's profession of tilling the
ground a sign of earthly and cupidinous mentality, little else was made of
the fact that the two brothers pursued different occupations. Legend
sought reasons for this distinction, however, since it was the difference in
professions that determined the nature of their offerings to God; and since
one of these offerings was unacceptable, the early thinkers were preoc-
cupied with why the brothers differed in work in the first place. The
apocryphal Book of Adam and Eve[9] provides details typical of the
extra-biblical legend that arose. After a dream in which Eve sees her elder
son murder his brother and drink his blood, the parents decide to avoid the
realization of the prophecy by separating their children, and Adam chooses

two different occupations for them. The theme of blood drinking and blood taboo generally is strongly present throughout the Cain tradition.

In dealing with the enigmatic problem of why Cain's offering was not pleasing to God, many commentators looked to the possible significance of the two occupations of the donors. Abel's role as the first shepherd and, moreover, the sacrificed shepherd was immediately seen as prefiguring the role of Christ as the Good Shepherd, further strengthening Cain's identification with the enemies of Christ. Cain's tilling of the same soil that had so recently been cursed through Adam's sin suggested blasphemy and cupidity. Josephus, a major influence on Bede, describes the inferiority of Cain's profession in terms of its being contrived and complicated: 'This was the offering [Abel's] which found more favour with God, who is honoured by things that grow spontaneously and in accordance with natural laws, and not by the products forced from nature by the ingenuity of grasping man.'[10] Curiously, farming was considered a means of cupidinous gain by the early Christian writers; herding – since animals, they believed, were not eaten in post-lapsarian society – was not.[11]

After his expulsion from human society, Cain continued to labour towards evil ends, originating all those activities that medieval man associated with the acquisitive appetite and the pernicious complication of society: 'He put an end to that simplicity in which men lived before by the invention of weights and measures: the guileless and generous existence which they had enjoyed in ignorance of these things he converted into a life of craftiness. He was the first to fix boundaries of land and to build a city, fortifying it with walls and constraining his clan to congregate in one place. This city he called Anocha after his eldest son Anoch.'[12] To the medieval mind treasuring the myth of a golden age in which nature was not perverted through empirical and quantitative devices and in which human society was universal, undivided, and uncircumscribed, such charges were serious indeed. For herein is ascribed to Cain the origin of every socially evil concept and the reverses that beset the Christian mission from the beginning. Two things, we may suppose, are evil about weights and measures to the medieval mind. First of all, they assign an arbitrary and unnatural characteristic to the thing measured, and these characteristics give it a false objective existence as 'thing.' Secondly, they presuppose division and consequent loss of integrity and wholeness. Similarly with boundaries, cities, and kinships: these lend a divisive and false identity contrary to what medieval man thought of as natural identity; they define by negation and exclusion and introduce self-consciousness, the very evil experienced by Adam and Eve when they chose 'to know.'

The Christian middle ages found this idea of natural simplicity not only in commentary such as that of Josephus but also in the classic writers who provided such a tradition. Vergil, with whom the Anglo-Saxons seem to have been quite familiar,[13] describes a golden age in which exactly those complications that the Christians thought Cain introduced were blissfully unknown: 'Before Jove held sceptre, no toiler subdued the land; even to mark the plain, or apportion it by boundaries, was crime; all that men gained was gained for the common stock; and Earth, unbidden, gave the more freely of her store, in that none asked her bounty.'[14] Cain, then, became an essential metaphor in primary conflict – a tension between two ways of looking at reality – and in defence of their Christian allegorical vision, medieval thinkers used this metaphor to represent the inferior perception.

Several ideas were advanced as to why God mysteriously rejected Cain's offering. The traditional vice of stinginess attached to Cain arises from speculation that he offered a grudging portion; the septuagint gave the hint for this in stating that Cain's offering was well brought but ill divided. Others viewed the failure as one of quality, not quantity, and asserted that he offered the worst of his crop.[15] But much later commentary emphasized the fact that the offering was from the cursed earth,[16] some going as far as to suggest that Cain offered back to God the very thorns the earth had been cursed to yield as a punishment for Adam's sin. Thus avarice, greed, and blasphemy were added to the already dim portrait of this archetypal villain.[17]

As early as the first-century Clementine epistles there is expressed the idea of Cain's murderous act as a further step in human decadence and the beginning of rebellion, violence, and war. While Adam and Eve had indeed fallen and subjected the human race to toil and death, it was thought that without Cain's sin man might have lived in relative innocence and simplicity in his post-Eden existence. With Cain's attack on his brother, however, began the history of enmity between brothers and all the specific evils that have ever plagued society.[18] Envy was seen as pre-eminent in Cain's motive for murder, as it had been in Satan's temptation of Eve,[19] and the hatred borne by Cain for Abel was seen as the envious hatred by the evil of the good simply because they are good.

It was not only the horror of the act itself, nor the violation of kinship, as horrible as it was, that impressed the medieval mind, but equally the fact that Cain's act was the very first occasion of the spilling of human blood and that by which death was introduced into the world. Thus Cain is pre-eminently the father of murder in tradition and by careful exegetical extension the inventor of war. Cain provides the grim precedent for all history, for as he was the first to destroy his brother through envy and hatred, so since then the chronicles of the greatest states have been filled with treason and fratricide.[20] St Ambrose thus interprets the scriptural reference to the origin of death: ' "Death came into the world through the evil of Satan" (Wisdom 2:24) He persuaded Cain to spill the blood of his brother in hateful envy. But Cain doubtless devoured his own soul with envy first, as much as other flesh, for as Scripture says: "Whoever hates his own brother is a murderer" (1 John 3).'[21]

The full significance of Cain's fratricide is seen, then, as an act determining the course of human history and repeated throughout history by human imitation of Cain in envy, anger, greed, and bloodshed. In this moral dimension of history Cain originates a certain type of evil, and his tropological 'descendants' perpetuate it. In the time of *Beowulf* it is Grendel's mother by whom 'cearu wæs geniwod' (1303) and 'sorh is geniwod' (1322), and through the dragon 'wroht wæs geniwod' (2287), suggesting, one might postulate, not only the renewal of local battles but the historical struggle itself. The same phrase is used by Wulfstan to describe the original contention: 'Heora bearna an gedyde syððan eac þurh deofles lare deoflice dæde, þæt wæs Cain. He ofsloh Abel, agenne broðor, 7 ða wæs Godes yrre þurh ða dæde ofer eorðan yfele geniwod.'[22]

The curse of Cain received much attention and lengthy explanation in commentary, all of it reflecting the divergence of the Vulgate from the Septuagint. The revelation of Cain's crime and the ensuing punishment is brought on by the calling out of Abel's blood from the earth that it drenched. The earth is seen to be involved in the curse in several ways: it receives the violated blood and is itself thus violated; it refuses its fruits to the murderer;[23] and never again does it afford Cain an abode. Thus a feature of the curse is his wandering.

As the earth stands for nature itself in the story, we see that it is nature that is violated in the drinking of human blood and rendered impotent. As a consequence of such unnaturalness, the perpetrator of the act is divorced from all natural relations. The idea of Cain's unnaturalness and his separation from the natural is the basis for the representation of him – and his descendants – as monster.[24] The peculiar symbolic and allegorical force of monsters in the middle ages is their representation of the unnatural and, with evil monsters, the anti-natural. The Christian concept of nature as the divine act of creation renders Cain a symbol of anti-creation. In his attack on the human community, which has its basis in nature, he looms as the particular symbol of that force against society and its creative foundation.[25]

Another feature of the curse is Cain's exile,[26] interpreted as an exile from all human community and intercourse and thought appropriate to his crime and any similar crime. Thus the standard penalty for parricide in medieval law is exile, frequently elaborated by references to Cain. Bede describes Cain's curse as exile, a state of physical unrest, and the loss of a peaceful home: 'Thirdly [he was condemned] to be forever a wanderer over the earth and an exile, and never to dare to hold a peaceful seat anywhere ...'[27]

St Augustine, too, associates the trembling of Cain with the crime he committed and considers it a punishment worse than death: 'In Cain the sin of fratricide appears truly in all its horror, and the scoundrel is consistent in being equally horrible ... And when he heard that the earth would bear forth nothing for his labours, and that he would be a wretch trembling and shaking over the earth, he would well have sought death who had invented it for his brother, but no one would give it to him.'[28] The sign of Cain was usually seen as identical to his curse, namely the trembling of his limbs and his exile. Its purpose was universally viewed not as a protection of his life, that he might enjoy existence, but instead as an extraordinarily long penance, that his suffering might be prolonged.[29]

The specific prohibition that Cain possess a permanent abode or 'peaceful seat' ('sedes quietas'), so often encountered in commentary, would seem to be identical with the idea of exile and wandering but may perhaps have been meant to indicate something more, for it was passed on verbatim through commentary. Its origin is possibly English, as Bede seems to be the earliest writer to use it.[30] The same idea is found at about the same time and place in Alcuin's *Interrogationes et Responsiones in Genesin*: '"What is the sign that God placed upon Cain that he might not be killed?" Answer: "That sign seems to have been that he would live forever an exile and a wanderer, trembling and shaking; nor would he ever dare to hold for himself a peaceful seat anywhere on the face of the earth."'[31]

Rabanus Maurus at about the same time also connects the mark of Cain with his curse, and like Bede and Alcuin he further associates it with Cain's inability to hold power of a 'peaceful seat.'[32] Several commentators in the ninth and tenth centuries pick up the formula to explain Cain's fate, and given the fact that some originality, at least, marks the Cain exegesis from century to century, one wonders whether some special significance in Cain's inability to attain a 'seat' was not recognized.[33] The Old Saxon

Genesis has a description of the same phenomenon fully within this tradition but contains the more precise image of Cain's exile as one from the comitatus:

> Fluhtik scalt thu thoh endi freðig. forwardas nu
> libbean an thesum landa, so lango so thu thit liaht waros;
> forhuaton sculon thi hluttra liudi, thu ni s(c)alt io furthur
>   cuman te thines herron sprako,
> we(h)slean thar mid wordon thinon.

(A fugitive and a wanderer shalt thou now henceforth live in this land, so long as thou shalt endure the light. Good people shall curse thee; thou shalt not ever again come to the assembly of thy lord, exchange there thy words.)[34]

Various bizarre conjectures also existed as to the nature of the sign that Cain bore, beginning with the Hebrew tradition, which proved very persistent, that it was a pair of horns. As Emerson has pointed out,[35] this idea found its way into Christian lore and is clearly seen in the religious drama of the Middle English period. Peter Comestor saw the sign as a trembling head, while Hugh of St Victor has a particularly vivid description of it as a frenzied, raging, spastic shaking of the entire body. Other suggestions include the protuding of horns from the nostrils, the association of his sign with circumcision, and sparkling, shiny eyes. Many of the minor exegetical characteristics took on somewhat more important status in folklore.

Cain's abode after his crime as described in exegesis is important in that one perceives herein a clear analogy to the terrain occupied by monsters in general in the later medieval descriptions. Again, a slight discrepancy in the scriptural rendition of Cain's dwelling provided a certain motive for innovation among the commentators, one stating that the fratricide went out to dwell in Nod, over against Eden; the other that he went to the east side of Eden, an exile on earth. Neither went far in providing details of the place of exile.

The name of Nod itself was thought to be as much a descriptive term as a proper name, as we see in the etymological interpretation of St Jerome: 'In Hebrew "Naid" is called "Nod" and it is translated σαλευόμενος, that is, unstable and changing, an uncertain seat.'[36] The chief characteristics of Cain's place of exile were that it was a desert place, a waste, solitary, and dark. Many of the characteristics of the description of Cain rest on the idea of the first murderer as the antithesis of light.[37] St Ambrose seems to see

Cain's antipathy to light and his seeking of a shadowy dwelling as expressive of the state of his soul: 'He hides himself, however, who would conceal and bury his sin. He who does evil hates the light and seeks out shadows and a lair for his crimes.'[38]

As well as a place of shadows Cain was thought to have sought out a dwelling among the beasts, an idea of prime importance for the later monster tradition. This idea likely arose out of the logical inference that since Cain was exiled from all human society then existing, the only company he could possibly have had in Nod was that of animals. In addition to its logic, the idea recommended itself on metaphorical grounds since it suggested that morally Cain had become a beast who had turned against his own kind. The bestiality of Cain's soul seems to be St Ambrose's suggestion in his description of Cain's refuge among the animals: 'He [the Lord] repulsed him from his countenance and, since he had violated his kin, he relegated him to a separate habitation in exile; there he was converted from human ways to the savagery of beasts.'[39]

Related to Cain's abode was the city he built, and exegesis is extreme in its condemnation of this act as a further and significant step in the corruption of society. On the one hand it was considered as a singularly impious attempt on Cain's part to defy the exile placed upon him by God. But more significant in the moral history of mankind, Cain's inauguration of city dwelling was looked upon as the beginning of an invidious complication of human society, its divorce from the innocent state of nature in the wake of which followed the development of his other divisions: borders, weights and measures, alchemy, magic, political states, tools, weapons, and wars. 'Firstborn of the first pair. As murderer C[ain] marks a further stage in the downward course of the fallen race, while he foreshadows its material progress.'[40]

The construction of the city is also closely identified with Cain's crime of fratricide, as is demonstrated by St Jerome in his description of the first architect: 'Further, it may be said that because Cain, the first parricide, built a city in the name of Enoch, his son, the Lord would not enter therein, for it was built on sin, blood, and parricide.'[41]

By far the most famous treatment of Cain's city is St Augustine's *City of God*, in which it is described as a physical representation of the dwelling in earthly and material things allegorically founded when Cain spilt his brother's blood: 'He who inaugurated the earthly city was a fratricide, for through envy he murdered his brother, a citizen of the eternal city while a pilgrim on earth.'[42]

The Bible does not identify Cain's wife and mentions her only in an enigmatic way: 'Cain knew his wife' (Genesis 4:17). The reason, of course, for later concern over the identity of Cain's mate is that Scripture seems to indicate that after the murder of Abel there were only three people left on earth. One of the solutions of exegesis was to assume the existence of a daughter of Adam whose birth went unrecorded due to her sex and whom Cain took as his wife.[43] Alternate explanations gained more currency in folklore than in exegesis, and they included two possibilities, one more repugnant than the other to the orthodox commentator. Thus the basis of the idea of the 'unholy pair' is created in the deduction that since there was only one woman in creation, it was his own mother who served as Cain's wife and through whom his line began. This theory gained enough currency to provoke Augustine to repudiate it. The other theory was that since there was no woman available to him, Cain sired his progeny upon the animals with which he lived in exile and thereby created the monstrous natures for which his descendants were famous.[44]

As has been mentioned, it was these descendants who passed on and developed the evil arts Cain had discovered, while adding several more. Clement I, in describing the unhallowed intercourse between angels and women of Cain's kin, saw the mixed nature of the fruit of this intercourse as possessing the ability to develop the questionable arts of metalwork, mining of precious gems, magic, and astronomy.[45] Other commentators emphasized the allegorical nature of descending from Cain in claiming that all those who imitated his evil were morally his brothers.[46] However, the historical dimension of Cain's progeny also occupied the minds of all exegetes since the accuracy of the story as history was crucial to the larger meaning. The particular significance of the generations of Cain begins with the sons of Lamech described in Scripture as inventors of three symbolic pursuits: Jabal, the origin of those who keep cattle; Jubal, the father of musicians; and Tubal-Cain, the inventor of metalwork, born of Lamech's second wife, Zillah.[47]. The three occupations suggest three types and perhaps stages of society – the agricultural, the urban, and the technological. The middle ages saw them, as well, as signs or types of harmony – or, more correctly, disharmony – existing in an evil epoch. The keeping of cattle suggested, because man already had begun to eat meat, disharmonious or imbalanced concern with the body. Jabal's descendants were nomads, further suggesting the state of exile so dreadfully viewed in the middle ages. As music in the middle ages was the symbol of harmony or disharmony depending on its mathematical arrangement, the music of Jubal connoted disharmony of the mind. Tubal-Cain's metalwork in brass and iron, specified in commentary as producing weaponry, was seen as a disharmony of the will in its leading to war. Thus the progeny of Cain represent the corruption of body, mind, and will.

The activity of the first smith is especially significant when related, as it always was, to Cain. Cain had been the first murderer, first to shed human blood, and according to tradition he thus originated not only homicide but war, as well, and all forms of blood-lust.[48] Just as his ancestor had taken the first step in the post-lapsus degeneration of the race, so Tubal-Cain continues the process in inventing the weapons by which Cain's particular evil could be effected. Tubal-Cain also prefigures the giants of Genesis 6 in his physical strength and prowess.[49]

The evil of the race of Cain was essential to historical tradition because it furnished certain moral-historical explanations for later events in Scripture and related them in an integrated manner. One such was the Flood. The degree of evil that called forth the Flood was immeasurable, and the direct cause of that evil according to exegesis ws the giants of Genesis 6.[50] The association of the family of Lamech with those giants was irresistible, both because of the proximity of their stories in Genesis and because of the meaningfulness of the association.[51] Searching for the continuity of the history of man and an explanation for the reversals in God's plan, the medieval thinker found here a key. Man's destiny had been thwarted in Eden, God's intention in the New Covenant had been deterred, and tyranny had characterized man's history. Even after the coming of the Messiah, the story of man had been one of bloodshed and lust. Discovering a unity and continuity in this dismal spectacle served to reinforce the unity and continuity of the positive forces of history as described in Christian doctrine. Thus Satan's success in Eden was continued in the decisive historical-ethical act of Cain, whose own descendants, present at so many significant historical moments of Old Testament history, carry on and perfect his malicious traditions. In the Anglo-Saxon *Genesis* a clear indication that bloodshed and fratricide, Cain's crimes, brought on the deluge emphasized Cain as the ultimate explanation of God's anger:

Næfre ge mid blode   beodgereordu
unarlice   eowre þicgeað,
besmitten mid synne   sawldreore.
Ælc hine selfa   ærest begrindeð
gastes dugeðum   þæra þe mid gares orde
oðrum aldor oðþringeð.   Ne ðearf he þy edleane gefeon
modgeþance,   ac ic monnes feorh
to slagan sece   swiðor micle,

and to broðor banan,   þæs blodgyte,
wællfyll weres   wæpnum gespedeð,
morð mid mundum   (1518–28)[52]

Lamech, as a true son of Cain, commits parricide for the second time in history whereby the first parricide himself meets death. Tubal-Cain, who in popular tradition directed the blind Lamech to fire the arrow that killed Cain, then becomes the first smith and inventor of tools for killing. While according to Genesis another line of righteous men was developing through Seth, beside them prospered a tribe dedicated to evil. Not only was the continuity of moral history impressive up to this point, but in relation to later events in Genesis it was seen as exceptional in its ability to weld the entire historical and moral content of Genesis into a related pattern based upon the significance of Cain and Seth.[53]

It was considered significant that Cain's genealogy ceased to be recorded at a given point. That point coincides with his own death in the seventh generation and the rise of the giants. Exegesis is unanimous in viewing the giants as descendants of Cain through 'the daughters of men'; disagreement persisted, as already mentioned, over the identity of 'sons of God,' Jewish and early Christian commentators often seeing them as fallen angels.[54] Later exegesis tended to allegorize the spiritual parentage of the giants and call them demons of pride and bloodthirstiness. So Augustine has it: 'It is possible therefore that giants were born even before the sons of God, who were also called the angels of God, united with the daughters of men, that is, of those who lived according to man, or, in other words, before the sons of Seth united with the daughters of Cain.'[55] Scripture itself lent great support to the allegorical view, for this interpretation seemed to lead to the statement of St John: 'In this the children of God are manifest, and the children of the devil; whoever does not righteousness is not of God, neither he that loveth not his brother. For this is the message that ye heard from the beginning, that we should love one another. Not like Cain, who was of the wicked one' (1 John 3: 10–11).

St Augustine insists that the difference between the two races of Genesis 6 is purely of moral disposition, not of human nature. He further claims the impossibility of the mixture of human and angelic natures and states not only that giants could have been naturally born but that indeed it continues to happen.[56] This interpretation seems also to lay unusual stress on the fact that there existed not only giant men but giant women, in an effort, perhaps, to create the possibility of a succession of naturally born giants.[57]

In England the 'sons of God' reading prevailed along with a tendency to preserve both the historical and the allegorical sense of the monsters.

Whereas Gregory the Great lays stress on the symbolic dimension of the designation 'gigantes' in his *Moralium*,[58] we see in Alcuin's *Interrogationes et Responsiones in Genesin* a successful balance of the literal and symbolic in the description of the monsters that arose from the union of the progeny of Cain and Seth. The confusion in the manuscript between Seth and Sem (Shem) and Cain and Cham is interesting in relation to the alleged confusion of the same nature in *Beowulf*.[59] There can be no doubt, however, that Alcuin is talking here about the races of Cain and Seth:

Concerning which it has been said: 'When man began to be multiplied over the earth ... (*Genesis* VI, 1–2). The progeny of Cain [ms Cham] is the daughters of men; and Scripture wishes to indicate that the offspring of Seth [ms Sem] are the sons of God. They have an ancestral religious blessing. These others of lewd parentage have a curse. And afterwards, the sons of Seth were overcome by concupiscence and joined in marriage with the daughters of Cain; and through such a union were procreated men of immense size, arrogant men of mixed natures, whom Scripture calls giants.[60]

Aelfric's translation of Scripture into Anglo-Saxon reveals the same view.[61]

Thus the giants of Genesis 6 were connected with the descendants and history of Cain as given in Genesis 4 and became his most illustrious progeny and perhaps the most spectacular feature of the tradition. The giants were creatures surrounded by mystery and wonder, although thought of as entirely human in origin and historic in character. Nevertheless they never quite lost their connection to the apocryphal legend of angelic parentage,[62] and the supernatural quality is likely attributable to this. In a moral sense they were equally exceptional, and the concept of giants as the ultimate progeny of Cain possessed both a literal-historic and an allegoric sense.

In addition to these views of the progeny of Cain supplied by Scripture and its exegesis, there was another dimension to the tradition of Cain's descendants. In the essentially literary embellishments of the scriptural story of the Flood, humanist commentators did not hesitate to connect the giants of Genesis 6 with the giants of classical myth who warred against the gods,[63] seeing in these pagan reports a corroboration, although erroneous in detail, of the historical verity of the scriptural account. Other myth, as well, was added to the story of Cain's life and progeny and their progress on earth, so that not only giants but every other species of monster was seen to be his child:

Adam had commanded his children, upon their lives to avoid certain herbs, that they might not thereby degenerate in their nature; his command they [these evil descendants of Cain] disregarded, their nature they lost. The children which they bore were various; some had heads like a dog, some had mouths on their breasts, eyes on their shoulders, and had to live without heads; some covered themselves with their ears, wonderful it is to hear. Some had one foot which was great and large, who straightway ran into the wood like a beast; some brought forth children that walked on all fours like cattle. Some lost altogether their beautiful complexion; they became black and terrible, there was nothing like them; their eyes were gleaming all the time, the teeth in their mouths were long; whenever they showed them they frightened the devil. Such life left the abandoned ones to all those who came after them; whatsoever inner nature the former had, such an outer nature the latter had to have. (Middle High German *Genesis*)[64]

These are, of course, the personae of the Book of the Monsters genre, with its own sources reaching to Pliny, Vergil, and several Christian writers, most eminently Augustine and Isidore; but unlike that genre, exegesis and popular legend gave these creatures a solid historical lineage and, in doing so, a capacity for allegorical meaning. All monsters in the middle ages are believed to descend from Cain, the giants being preeminent in that descent, but sirens or dragons, should they be met with, also fall into this kinship, for only through this rational and historical perspective could they have moral meaning and a place in the philosophic system. Their historic integrity was assured through the ability of exegesis to link the several gigantic figures of the Old Testament together. The propriety of such connections was more than excused by the significantly similar stories of moral depravity surrounding these figures.

Nimrod was the first of the post-diluvian giants mentioned in Scripture, and it was considered significant that he is the grandson of Ham, agent of the giants by tradition. Nimrod shares many of the characteristics of the monsters of literary tradition, being black, like those who lost their complexions through sin, bloodthirsty, strong, and beastlike. So he is described by St Ambrose through interpretation of his name: 'Nimrod by etymological interpretation is called "the Ethiopian." The colour of an Ethiopian signifies the squalor of a dark soul, which is the enemy of light, deprived of brightness, wrapped in shadows, more like the night than the day. He was a hunter in the woods, and his society was among wild beasts.'[65] Moreover, he specifically commits the crime of Cain in becoming the founder of an even more infamous city, Babylon. He is a hunter and thus a dealer in blood, the crime most constantly associated with the giants. The historical continuity of his city is seen in its connection to Sodom and Gomorrah through the Canaanites. The genealogy is continued through the Philistines to Goliath, the last of the famous giants, defeated by David, God's chosen ruler of Israel.

Between Nimrod and Goliath there was a clear and direct historical connection, and to the medieval mind this continuity of the giant family was vivid and real. According to St Augustine, Og, who was king of Basan, was one of the Raphaim, or giants, of the Old Testament. The Enacim, another name for giants, controlled the ancient kingdom of Azotus, now Palestine.[66]

The allegorical continuity was also attended to since each figure was interpreted as morally significant. Nimrod, as we have seen in St Ambrose's quite typical description, is perceived as a rapacious hunter and dweller in shadows, connoting his inherited blood-lust and hatred of truth. Tubal-Cain, his ancestor, also a mighty man and hunter, is seen as earthly and sensuous, having forged metal from the bowels of the earth itself to fashion the tools by which creatures might be slain and then devoured.[67] Goliath, the Philistine, is the symbol of huge pride and the filth that characterized the enemies of Israel. Specifically denoted as uncircumcised, he is the archetypal outsider menacing the elite.[68] Thus the giants in their carnivorous habits represent the inordinate sensuality of depraved man. In their intimate association with cities and monuments, as well as their own size, they express the monumental dimensions of fallen human pride, the origin of all evil. The human condition, both in its historical manifestation and in its personal expression, found a full and appropriate symbol in the far-flung kinship of the monsters and giants descended from 'the depravity which is every-dying but never dead, whose name is Cain.'[69]

The characteristics of the progeny of Cain formed the descriptive aspect of the monster tradition. Their sinfulness was both general and specific since the idea of their mixed natures created an impression of general depravity, but their historical and genealogical origins encouraged assignment of specific crimes. Thus all unnatural malevolence was associated with Cain and his descendants. As early as the first century it was thought and stated by churchmen that Cain's progeny possessed the power of the shape shifter and could become at will quadrupeds, serpents, birds, or fish, or whatever else they wished.[70] This type of exegesis forms an important philosophical element in the whole genre of the grotesque and is one of the conceptual bases of the aesthetic use of monsters in the middle ages.

Further, as the sinfulness of Cain's race was closely associated with the world-wide evil that preceded the Flood, those giants and monsters were also associated with pagan deities. Just as St Augustine had attributed social disharmony throughout history to the Cain-like spirit of paganism manifested in its gods, generally these monsters were seen as personifying social chaos. Thus Justin Martyr declared in the second century that these monsters lead men into slavery, into the practice of magic and of idolatry resulting in war and social evils.[71] This idolatry was particulary connected to the figures of monster and giant, and they were seen as continuing a war against God that began with Cain:

They [Christian writers] pointed to the Greek myth [Jove and the giants] as not only confirming Scripture, but explaining in a simple manner the whole basis of the heathen mythologies. The giants who warred against Jove were the giants of Scripture, who opposed God and wrought wickedness. They and their descendants became heathen gods, who were thus not gods at all, but wicked men or devils. The early Fathers connected these heathen gods with the giants of *Genesis 6*, so that they were thus descendants of Cain.[72]

Thus could the world be filled with monsters.

One of the salient characteristics of these giants and monsters in tradition was their abode. They were to be found among the beasts and, although hunters, held social intercourse among animals. Much commentary clearly suggests that the object of their hunt was human flesh. The Clementine *Homily 8* describes the giants as detesting pure food because of their double nature. They first among mankind tasted flesh and introduced the habit to man. However, when animals ran short, they began with their followers to eat human flesh. As Cain was the first to shed human blood, his descendants advanced his degeneracy in introducing cannibalism. The abode of these cannibalistic monsters was regularly specified as either underground or underwater.

It is probably from the scriptural account of the Flood that the tradition of an underwater home arose. As has been said, it was exegetical tradition that the destruction of the world by water was caused by the evil of the giants. The survival of evil after the Flood required some explanation. The reappearance of a hunter and 'mighty man' in the figure of Nimrod illustrated the fact of survival of the monsters but did not explain it. Commentators quickly noticed that one, at least, of the ark's passengers had not been a paragon of justice. His sinful action directly after the establishment of the new society proved Ham a corrupt man; and, as has already been stated, there existed a popular tradition that Ham had been instructed in the evil arts of the giants prior to the Flood and had inscribed formulae on stones that would not be obliterated by waters. After the Flood he returned to these monuments of evil and, as the agent of Cain and the giants, began to reintroduce evil ways into the world. This is the important tradition reported by Cassian in the fourth century:

How it happened that the knowledge of strange things of which we have spoken did not disappear with the Flood, but survived in following ages, should be explained ... Ancient tradition tells us that Ham son of Noah, who had been instructed in these superstitions, profane, and sacrilegious arts, knew he could not bring a book on these subjects into the ark in which he was to go with his righteous father and holy brothers. So he carved these evil arts and profane writings on various metals and hard stones which could not be worn away by the water. When the deluge was finished he searched them out with the same curiosity with which he had hid them and transmitted to posterity the seeds of sacrilege and profanity ... From these sons of Seth and daughters of Cain there were born more iniquitous offspring who became mighty hunters, most violent and truculent men who because of their physical enormity, cruelty, and evil were called hunters.[73]

Such an explanation provided the historical connection the middle ages desired, for it joined Ham to the race of Cain and related the new evils to the old heritage of immorality. Ham began to revive the evil of Cain after the Flood, and his two sons, Cush and Mizraim, aided him in re-establishing the monster race. Cush became father of Nimrod and Mizraim gave rise to the nation of the Philistines, finally producing Goliath.

The tradition of the descent of the monsters from Cain and Ham is the subject of apparent confusion in the middle ages. Especially in Britain, the descent of the monsters is referred to Cain. Moreover as we have seen, several descriptions of Genesis 1–4 identify the villain not as Cain but as Ham. Most interesting to the present study is the example of this phenomenon in *Beowulf*. According to Donahue in 'Grendel and the Clanna Cain,' a similar 'confusion' exists, but he asserts that the more orthodox explanation of Cain as progenitor of monsters is behind this later Old Irish tradition, and the Irish Ham legend is apparently the result of a conscious effort of literal-minded exegetes.

Further James Carney makes a strong case for the theory that the author of *Beowulf* had intimate knowledge of Irish folk literature and exegesis.[74] He specifically identifies Isidore of Seville's *Etymologiae* as an influence on *Beowulf* through the Irish *Sex Aetates Mundi*, which was heavily indebted to Isidore. Thus for Carney the Ham-Cain 'confusion' is reflective more likely of doctrinal stance than of incomplete knowledge.

While it is indeed possible that the manuscript difficulty in *Beowulf* is related to Irish exegesis and doctrine, it is well to remember that the Ham legend as such is far older than the *Sex Aetates Mundi*, and that whatever its origin, the transposition of Ham for Cain – and Shem for Seth – was not restricted to *Beowulf*. In any case, it is very unlikely that the author *Beowulf*, or any other Anglo-Saxon writer, really thought Ham was Cain, or that Cain was not related to the origin of monsters. As Carney points out, 'the author of *Beowulf* obviously gave Cain as the ancestor of monsters.'[75] A possible reason why Ham and Cain could be interchanged as the origin of monsters and monstrous crime is that Ham is seen as the agent by whom the evil originated by Cain in an earlier time is reintroduced into a new world, the post-diluvian world of the Second Covenant. An author highly sensitive to the schemes of the ages of man and atuned to the symbolism of the Flood and the ark as destruction and new creation might well have given the name Ham in place of Cain in order to signify the reintroduction of evil into the newly cleansed world. He would nevertheless be counting on the ability of his audience to connect this evil ultimately to Cain.

Beyond historical detail the symbolic force of the story of the origin of monsters was meant to express the reality that the evil introduced by the first fratricide survived, and that those who practised such evil became monstrous members of his race. The first-century Clementine Homilies contain a description of the law that is placed on the surviving monsters to keep them within tolerable limits but which recognizes that those human beings who shed blood are to be counted as among the worshippers of the giants.[76]

More significantly, the basic vehicle of Augustine's most important historical work, *The City of God*, was that of two moral and spiritual traditions in which it is seen that all evil-doers by the choice of evil over good became citizens of that city founded by the first fratricide, the city that transcends history and exists in all times. Thus not only are all monsters related to Cain as personifications of antisocial and unnatural forces, but all men who are unnatural enough to hate their brothers and who weaken the state and undermine social harmony by lust and ambition are also Cain's descendants. In this way not only giants but all those 'monsters' associated with social disaster were seen as descended from Cain.

The extension of the concept of Cain-descended monster was such as to include not only ordinary men who followed in the way of the giants, but also various beasts in specific form whose allegorical connotation allowed them to be related to Cain and his crimes. The most significant for the study of *Beowulf* is the relation of the dragon to the first fratricide.

Gregory the Great in the sixth century directly associates the dragon with Cain: '"I was a brother to dragons and a companion to ostriches." What is there denoted by "dragons," but the life of malicious men? ... He refuses to be Abel whom the evil of Cain does not distress.'[77] Throughout medieval tradition the dragon was interpreted as the Devil in monster guise, based upon the form that Satan adopted to seduce Eve. In this manifestation he is Leviathan, and the symbol is expressive not of generalized evil but of a malice more particular. Whether it be Ladon or the Beast of the Apocalypse, the evil dragon[78] is identified with time and the disruption of order.[79] In the story of St George the dragon is the enemy of civilization represented by the city and the force of chaos represented by his emerging from a cave. Once again we see here the medieval habit of assigning double and opposing significance to the same sign.

The symbolic force of the city in the legend of Cain is evil, representing complexity as contrasted to simplicity and even betokening the change from an unfallen world to a fallen one. In the legend of St George the city is a positive symbol, the metaphor of order against disorder. So the city, like Venus the mother of fornication and Venus the mother of regeneration, functions in the double manner. Thus chaos is related to the idea of unrestrained erotic energy, and the dragon emerges from a cavern , is subdued by a lance and, in several saints' legends, led in submission by a woman's girdle. In the later version of the St George story the ordered sexual union in marriage of the woman and the dragon slayer signifies the triumph of the city over the dragon. St Michael casts disorder and rebellion in the form of a dragon into the abyss. Daniel forces pitch, fat, and hair[80] into the cavernous throat of a dragon (Bel and the Dragon, 27), killing the monster and thereby converting the king and bringing true order to Babylon, symbol of chaos.[81]

While all monsters are descended, then, from Cain, his most infamous progeny are the giants and the dragon. Indeed, the dragon is in many ways more intimately associated with him, as Gregory the Great shows in describing Cain's murder of Abel as his succumbing to the fire of Leviathan: 'He [Leviathan] enflamed the mind of Cain with the fire of envy when he became aggrieved at the acceptance of his brother's sacrifice, and through this he went all the way to the sin of fratricide.'[82]

Christian ideology posited a redeemed world, a new covenant the laws of which were contained in Christian doctrine, and in which evil was banished from the world and virtue regenerated. That theory of virtue placed a high value on freedom from the material world and participation in a spiritual life of values led by the value of brotherhood. This ideology looked forward to a harmonious society governed by Christian social teaching and testifying to a progressive enlightenment of man through history, beginning with the covenant after the Flood and rebeginning with the coming of the Messiah. In this vision of men at harmony with one another and with nature, Christian apologists laid special emphasis on the ideals of peace, asceticism, simplicity, and love. But history, in fact, revealed no such progress, and instead disharmony, bloodshed, and materialism prospered in Christian and pagan societies alike. In face of historical reality the Christian propagandists and social writers developed the images of the contraries of the values they wished to promote in their war on evil: war and its instruments, blood, cannibalism, the fortified city, metals, and all divisive instruments such as weights, boundaries, and measuring tools.

Not only was it evident to many that no absolute progress could be seen in pagan societies as the time of the Messiah approached, but worse still, the social history of the Christian period gave little indication of a decisive movement towards freedom from the world and its vices. From the time of Christ cities grew up, wars raged, and material progress and devotion to it continued.

In regard to this problem a particular perspective of history was developed in which it was shown that from the beginning two movements in human history could be discerned, the one virtuous and essentially identical to Christianity, the other evil and a constant contradiction of Christianity. Augustine made the fullest and most famous expression of this view, although he did not invent it. Not only had Christian thinkers before him seen history in this way, but before them the Jews, too, had conceived history similarly in their claim to be the chosen people. Augustine's theory of history is another way in which the Christians took over to themselves the concept of the chosen people, an elite to which one belongs by moral choice and which is persecuted by the world. In face of the progress of the enemy, the virtuous society was inevitably compromised in this world and thus was forced to build its own cities and wage its own wars. The essential difference, however, was that the members of the virtuous society were merely pilgrims in the world of matter and reluctant participants in linear time whose spiritual ideals were quite other than their historical practices. In this spirit St Augustine, who is among those Christians who take the gravest view of violence, could say that what was reprehensible about war was not the death of its victims, whose fate it was to die in any case, but the spirit of enmity and bloodthirstiness by which they met their death.

In such a perspective the societies of the past and those of the present – pagan society and Christian society – are more similar than dissimilar. The races of the evil and of the good exist at all moments of time and in all places, and the virtuous pagans maintained generally the same struggle against the opponent as Christians, for indeed it was the same opponent. The complete distinction and difference between Christian and pagan seen from other Christian perspectives did not eliminate this continuity of evil and of good, and the analogy between the two societies remained purposeful.

For this perspective the story of Cain and Abel was seen as an ideal metaphor. Through exegetical embellishment and ideological reworking a tradition was developed, consonant with the facts of scriptural report, that drew out the meaning of these facts and extended them to an entire explication of psycho-moral history illuminating not only the past and present but the future, as well. Its function was, then, a most important one: to explain the lacunae and contradictions between Christian ideology and experiential reality.

The tropes of this tradition were the fratricide, the cannibal, the monster, the city, and the sword, all related to Cain. To the man of the eighth century surrounded by these symbols and their reality in his own Christian society, which theoretically rejected such violence, a symbolic system of doubles provided an answer to the apparent contradiction. In response to the city of Babylon, there was the spiritual city of Jerusalem; against the sword of enmity, the sword of justice; Seth as well as Cain. Part of the value of the particular perspective of the past in the Cain tradition is that it helps to solve the vexing conundrum of continuing evil. If indeed the past can be seen never to have been totally evil, then the present could be accepted as less than totally good. That is to say that in the view of history in the Cain tradition, the theory of progress is qualified and continuity emphasized, and through such readjustment the contradictions and lacunae of the Christian theory fade.

3

The Poetic Present and the Fabulous Mode

The allegorical structure of *Beowulf* involves two sets of double schemes: on the one hand an historical narrative related to a fabulous narrative; on the other hand an extension of present event to the future through prophecy and a related extension of present event to the past through allusion.[1] These two sets are related one to the other in possessing common elements. Thus in the present-historical mode we have Hrothgar and Beowulf in Denmark, Hygelac and Beowulf in Geatland. In the present-fabulous mode we have Beowulf and Grendel in Denmark and Beowulf and the dragon in Geatland.

The extension of present to future and present to past serves to illuminate the significance of both historical and fabulous event. The significance of Beowulf and Hrothgar in Denmark is thus clarified, for example, by a reference to a great Germanic hero of the past, Sigemund, and to the future in the allusion to Hrothulf's treachery. The full significance of events in Geatland is gradually illuminated by a series of references to past and to future, in the story of Haethcyn and that of the final destruction of the Geats under Wiglaf.

The elaboration of the interrelationship of these double sets leads to a perception of the theme of the poem as well as its structure. The key to this relationship is the figure of Cain, himself both historical and fabulous at one and the same time, and allegorically existing in present, past, and future. Thus, for instance, Sigemund's salient characteristics are his war with the 'eotena cyn' associated elsewhere in the poem with the giants of Genesis and kin of Cain, his battles with dragons, and his respect for human kinship. The reference to this hero apparently functions to highlight the heroic actions of Beowulf against the monsters, the core of the fabulous mode. At one level the interrelation of this historic narrative of Sigemund and the fabulous narrative of Grendel is fairly obvious: the central figures of both stories are prodigious heroes who defeat monsters. At a more fundamental level the interrelation can be see to be more complex and more thoroughgoing. Both are enemies of the 'eotena cyn,' have deep feelings for the bond of kinship and are the opponents of fratricide. These characteristics take on their full meaning only in the tradition of Cain, the archetypal fratricide who sired a race of monsters dedicated to the destruction of the kinship bond.

In contrast, the story of Hrothulf, alluded to in the poem as a future prediction and known to the audience as past history, is one of parricide and violation of kin whereby Hrothulf will usurp the throne from his cousins, likely with the assistance of Unferth, identified earlier in the poem as a fratricide. Similarly, the story of Haethcyn of Geatland provides another example of a fratricide in the past of the poem as well as the pathos of the spectacle of the unvengeable crime. The crime associated constantly with Cain in the middle ages is thus an eminent feature of the Geatish past and apparently is the occasion for Hygelac's ascension to the throne. In the allusion to the future of the Geats it is intimated that they will ultimately be destroyed by the Cain-like spirit of vengeance of Eadgils, who will strike at Wiglaf, son of the agent of Onela's parricidal murder of Eanmund, brother of Eadgils and nephew of Onela.

In such episodes the historical incident is invested with a tropological meaning through the employment of the metaphorical vocabulary of the tradition of Cain. The repetition of the theme in one historical allusion after another has the effect of universalizing this meaning. The story of Haethcyn is an example from the past – more specifically, from the past history of the Geatish royal house – while the story of Eadgils and Wiglaf is an allusion to the Geatish future. Both participate in the Cain tradition and the theme of parricide and vengeance, and in being in different temporal moments they show the extension of that theme to past and future. Similarly, the prediction of the fall of Heorot through parricide and the stories, for instance, of Heremod and Unferth extend the image of a socially ever-present Cain to the past and future of the Danes, yoking time and space in the universalization of the theme.

The opening of the poem presents to us the image suggestive of the setting in which the traditions of peace and of enmity began. Heorot as a psychological macrocosm and social microcosm distinguished by newness, innocence, and goodwill recalls almost irresistibly aspects of the

Garden of Eden. In addition, Heorot as symbol possesses a historical dimension as the sign of the Danes' greatest social achievement and the reign of peace, stability, and brotherhood in Denmark.

The description of Heorot is prefaced in the opening lines of the poem by a reference to the Danish past in which we find that, after suffering the dreaded state of lordlessness, the Danes found relief in the coming of Scyld, who founded a dynasty that provided a stable society right up to the time of the action of the poem and presently maintained by Hrothgar. Thus the Danes are conscious that their past has been marked by both misery and splendour, and that under Hrothgar it has reached its greatest height. As a symbol of this, Heorot is built.

It is difficult in the face of the text and the tone of the poem to accept Goldsmith's contention that Hrothgar is a victim of sinful pride and that Heorot symbolizes that sin.[2] While her thesis concerning the nature of the allegorical mode of *Beowulf* coincides to a great degree with the present argument, her description of the theme of the poem itself and the significance of its characters is less acceptable in light of the conclusions suggested by the present investigation. It is, for instance, difficult to agree with Goldsmith's perception of Heorot as a symbol of arrogance when the text seems to lead directly to another view. Not only has Hrothgar effected peace with foreign nations, a great Christian virtue and rare pagan achievement, but he has created harmony and brotherly love at home: 'þæt him his winemagas / georne hyrdon' (65–6). It is also evident that the king intends to use Heorot in a way consistent with the new social harmony, for there, we are told, he will reward that peace by performing the ceremony of the highest value in his society, the sharing of treasure. The way in which the poet insists on the moral aspect of the theme through the description of life in Heorot seems to support its identification as the symbol of the good society.

The identification of Heorot with Eden does not require us to overlook the clearly negative aspects of the hall. Unferth's fratricide, for instance, does not contradict the Eden image but largely completes it. As in Eden, the seeds of Heorot's fall are within it, and as Cain was a dweller in paradise, so is Unferth in Heorot. The hall as a symbol of peace comes into existence after a history of war and violence. The symbolic does not deny the historical, but the symbol cannot be read as historic account. To be sure, Heorot is as much a symbol of fallen Eden when the hall itself crumbles as it is of pre-lapsarian Eden while its social values are in force.

Particular emphasis would seem to be placed on the respect of virtues of kinship and generosity in Heorot. Hrothgar apparently rules with his nephew Hrothulf, with whom he seems to share the throne.[3] We have no reason to doubt that the king's motives are generous, and the poet lets Wealhtheow describe them as such. His granting of sanctuary to Ecgtheow and his settlement of the exile's feud would indicate that his generosity extends beyond members of his kin, as well.

It is only after the clear establishment of Hrothgar and Heorot as the embodiment of social virtue that the poet introduces their antithesis, the exiled monster descended from Cain who opposed Hrothgar and his hall and all they stand for. Grendel attacks Heorot because he is outlawed ('forscrifen') with Cain's family, a band dedicated to perpetuating their characteristic crime, the destruction of kin. Thus the court of Hrothgar representing kinship, peace, fidelity, and civilization is pitted against the forces of Cain: parricide warmongery, treason, and cannibalism.

Such a contrast makes it especially difficult to agree with Goldsmith's attribution of Grendel's motives for attacking Heorot to the pridefulness that she claims the hall represents.[4] The logial conclusion to such a view is to see Grendel as justified in his actions, indeed as an instrument of God. Cain, too, as exegesis makes clear, found Abel's piety insufferable, but that piety did not thus become pride, and Cain's motive was described as the hatred of good simply because it is good. Similarly, the poet would seem to have followed this assignment of motive in describing Grendel's inspiration as enmity.

The setting, then, of the poetic present in the first part of the poem is presented as the virtuous society of Hrothgar symbolized by Heorot. The main action that takes place in this setting is fabulous, and by this term we do not mean unreal, for Grendel and his attacks are vividly real and destructive. Instead the action of the poem, while occurring in time and space, involves figures and events of supranatural character having symbolic meaning. Just as the medieval Christian knew clearly that Samson, for instance, was a real, historic figure, he also recognized that he and his story were unusual and wondrous, and that they were so in order to convey a special meaning that they represented. Similarly, into the historic reality of Hrothgar's Denmark steps Grendel, the genealogical descendant of Cain and the symbolic force against the brotherhood of Hrothgar's court and the peace of all societies. Both Grendel's historic reality and his symbolic meaning derive from his relationship to Cain and are expressed through allusion to the exegetical tradition built up around Cain. His physical reality and moral significance are described by direct borrowings from that legend. Other characters in the poem, including Beowulf, are established by a technique of association and disassociation from Cain and Grendel in their actions.

Thus Grendel is described as a fiend of hell ('feond on helle,' 101) and bold demon ('ellengæst,' 86; 'grimma gæst,' 102), suggesting characteristics consonant with the exegetical description of Cain as Devil-sired and father of a line of evil creatures of mixed nature. Grendel is also designated as a giant ('þyrse,' 426), yet from other descriptions he does not seem very much bigger than his surroundings. It is possible that because of Grendel's association with the line of Cain the poet felt no incongruity in naming him among the giant progeny of that line. The nature of the giants in the tradition depended less on their physical size than on the immensity of their evil, and they are represented as ordinary creatures, though bigger than usual.[5]

The monster is also described as a cannibal, and given the genealogy supplied by the poet we can associate this characteristic with that of the brood of which he is one. Grendel's role as 'muthbona' (2079) of Hrothgar's thanes would seem to reinforce his paraticular association with the giants of Cain's descendancy, those who according to tradition first tasted flesh and, when the flesh of animals ran short, resorted to feeding off humankind.

Grendel is also described as 'wonsæli' (105) and 'sceadugenga' (703), and while both are frequent enough terms of descriptions, they seem peculiar in this context. One is prompted to ask why Grendel, renowned for his fierceness and completely victorious over the Danes, is also an 'unhappy creature' and a 'walker in shadows.' One possible answer lies in similar descriptions in the Cain tradition of the parricide's exile, which was regularly described as exile into a place of darkness. St Cyprian's description of Cain as 'a walker in shadows,'[6] borrowed from the epistle of St John, is the Latin equivalent of the Anglo-Saxon description of Grendel as 'sceadugenga' and is reminiscent of St Ambrose's description of Cain as hating light and desiring darkness: 'he hates the light and seeks out the shadows.'[7] Thus, like his ancestor, Grendel is a creature of darkness appearing in the poem either at night or in an undergound, lightless cave.

Grendel's opposition to Heorot is very strongly emphasized in the rhetoric of the description of his attack, the hall being specified as target six times in the eighteen lines describing his approach (702–20). The force against Heorot and its values is described as 'walker in shadows' (703), 'demonic enemy' (717), 'bearing God's wrath' (711), 'wicked demon' (712), and 'bereft of joy' (721). A further contrast between the monster and the hall is perhaps noticeable earlier in the description of his past ravages of

Hrothgar's society, in which Grendel, although a completely victorious enemy, is said to be ultimately unable 'to greet the gift-seat':

> No he þone gifstol   gretan moste,
> maþðum for Metode,   ne his myne wisse. (168–9)

One might well agree with Wrenn in his suggestion that the passage refers to Cain and is in that sense a continuation of line 110 describing Grendel's descent,[8] but it does not follow that the throne is therefore God's. The word 'gifstol' can be understood more generally as chair or seat, and can mean seat in an extended sense of city or habitation. This seems to be exactly the sense in the only other use of the word in the poem, 'gifstol Geata' (2327), home of the Geats.[9] In the sense that treasure was traditionally distributed in the king's 'city' and from his throne, that seat of government might well be described as a treasure, 'maþðum.' Thus the lines may possibly be understood: 'He could not attain a seat, that treasure, because of God's curse.' The intended contrast, then, between the formidable monster and the helpless Danes would be that, regardless of his force, Grendel could not belong to an established society as they, his victims, did. The monster, as a descendant of Cain, is an exile from social pleasures, and since exile is a punishment, it may be seen to cause suffering. This is a point made elsewhere by the poet when he describes Grendel alone in his lair listening to the communal sounds of Heorot and the scop's song of creation, and characterizes him as 'exiled' (100) and 'one against all' (145).

A recurrent feature of the traditional description of Cain's exile, as we have seen, was the prescription 'Sedes certas [or quietas] non habere.' This peculiar addition to exegetical tradition seems to have been English, as has been pointed out, and Bede seems to be its origin. There may well exist a relation between the terms 'sedes quietas' ('non habere'), with its connotation of wandering, and the *Beowulf* poet's 'gifstol' ('ne gretan'), in the sense of 'a society,' unapproachable to one of Cain's kin.

Grendel therefore is presented as the monstrous outsider enraged by the joys of brotherhood and society from which he is forever banished. Grendel's enmity towards Heorot is grounded solely in this moral perversion, another example of the hatred of the good simply because it is good. The poet seems to insist on this point with every adjective describing the two opposites and, of course, through the controlling phenomenon of the monster's descent from Cain, who committed the first murder simply out of envy.

The generalized contrast of Grendel with Heorot is that of the monster in opposition to the city, chaos against order, and it functions to express at once the vulnerability to which man feels his social creations are subject and his general fear of phenomenal nature. The hostile monster, then, is modelled on the Genesis myth, which describes an assault against man's initial efforts of socialization and in which Cain, the criminal, is punished in a way both symbolically appropriate to the offence and pragmatically effective in preventing the further weakening of society: he is exiled. Thus the second aspect of the idea, the fear of uncontrolled nature, is also seen in the punishment. Cain is 'outside'; Seth and Adam's other descendants, 'inside.' The medieval city repeats this contrast with its walls and moats beyond which lie the lawless forests and wastes into which are sent civil exiles, those beyond the full force of the law.

In general, then, the contrast of Grendel and Heorot is part of the widespread depiction of the monster as the uncontrolled force without, the perpetual threat to the order governing those who have come together in its name within the boundaries of the city, the castle, or the hall. This menace is depicted in *Beowulf*, as in other discussions of it, in fabulous form: it is a monster of prodigious strength, boundless fury, incomparable appearance. Its monstrosity defies nature, for nature cannot be seen to be outside the order that is threatened. As an expression of the enormity of the phenomenon, only the fabulous mode will permit a description inclusive of enough metaphorical characteristics to denote the monster's evil. Grendel, therefore, although a historical descendant of a scriptural-historical figure, is a fabulous being who engages in a series of fabulous actions of bloody malevolence. The opposition to him is by necessity of the same genre and takes place at the level of the fabulous. The destruction of disorder – on the fabulous level, Beowulf's defeat of Grendel – is nevertheless the means by which historical perspective is gained. The Christian vision of the middle ages, or for that matter of any civilization, was to extend, through its ideology, the boundaries demarcating order from chaos until spatially a single 'city' could be created around which no walls were needed because no territory would not be included; until ideologically a single standard of civilization was universally accepted and no ideological 'space' remained without.

The monster that attacks the city from without is thus regularly described in terms of animals, suggesting the irrational, which cannot profit from human order, but in such a way as to distinguish it from the natural animal, which is governed by its own form of law. This distinction is usually accomplished by the creation of a figure composed of disparate bodily parts – the beginning of the grotesque mode. Thus Grendel is presented as a figure recognizably human in several ways, but physically a grotesque composite of various animal parts. He is scaly – that is, his gloved claw that hung in Heorot was made of dragon's skin (2085) – he has claws, and he is possessed of enormous strength. His human aspect is presented by the poet not through physical description but by the depiction of his mental life, which is clearly rational. Instead of using the mythic mode employed in tales such as those of St George and the dragon or Theseus and the Minotaur, where the meaning of the conflict between man and monster is perceived in the action and its context, the *Beowulf* poet attributes motive and intention to the monster and has him express it in both thought and action, raising the conflict to an allegorical level on which rational principles fight for dominance, albeit in the fantastic style.

But the poet is here not content with a generalized allegory of evil against good, or even chaos against order, for the monster is further provided with an entire genealogy derived from historical and cultural legend that, without mitigating his symbolic force as monster-against-civilization, specifies it in the allegorical mode. As an additional detail of Grendel's grotesque appearance when he bursts into Heorot, the poet tells us of his fiery eyes:

> Him of eagum stod
> ligge gelicost   leoht unfæger. (726–7)

This characteristic, unlike his strength, size, and physical appearance, which have immediate force in and of themselves, is fully meaningful only in relation to an iconographic system, and such is found in the medieval monster tradition. The *Liber Monstrorum*, for instance, contains one example of monsters with shiny eyes: 'There is said to be a certain island in the eastern part of the world where men are born of rational appearance, except that from their eyes there shines a light.'[10] The origin of the tradition and its significance lie probably in the Cain tradition, which posited wild, gleaming eyes as the sign received by the first fratricide. Such is the idea to which Migne refers in his note to Peter Comestor's discussion of Cain.[11]

The relation of Cain to Grendel is provided by the poet at the outset of the poem. Grendel's genealogy is presented directly on the heels of the account of the activity at Heorot, described in lines 90–8 as the recitation of the story of God's creation of the world, as if to contrast the celebration of life at the hall with its opposite, for Grendel is found to be the direct historical descendant of the figure who introduced death to the world:

Wæs se grimma gæst   Grendel haten,
mære mearcstapa,   se þe moras heold,
fen ond fæsten;   fifelcynnes eard
wonsæli wer   weardode hwile,
siþðan him Scyppend   forscrifen hæfde
in Caines cynne –   þone cwealm gewræc
ece Drihten,   þæs þe he Abel slog;
ne gefeah he þære fæhðe,   ac he hine feor forwræc,
Metod for þy mane   mancynne fram.
Þanon untydras   ealle onwocon,
eotenas ond ylfe   ond orcneas,
swylce gigantas,   þa wið Gode wunnon
lange þrage;   he him ðæs lean forgeald. (102–14)

Grendel, then, is no generalized metaphor but a figure of historic dimension belonging to a large and variegated clan that includes all monsters and giants. He and his kinsmen are descendants of Cain and from their ancestor derive their salient characteristic and the symbolic force of the legend surrounding them. The role of Grendel in the poem cannot be evaluated outside of this legend, which the poet so clearly puts before his readers at the outset, and to a great degree the role of Beowulf as the opponent of this clan must also be defined in relation to his contrary, the descendants of Cain. The dramatic purpose of Beowulf's boast later on, in response to Unferth's taunt that he has successfully fought water monsters (575) and giants' kin (420–1), is probably to establish his credentials for doing battle with Grendel, a monster like those with whom he has already contended. Grendel, in fact, dwells with exactly the same type of monster Beowulf defeated in his swimming match, the 'nicor' (845). The word 'nicor' is derived from Old Norse 'nykr' and related to Old High German 'nihhus,' crocodile. 'Nicor' is thus related to the dragon and can perhaps be seen to prepare the audience for Beowulf's later battle in Geatland. The reference to giant-related monsters ('eotena cyn') more clearly prefigures the battles with Grendel, who is himself an 'eoten,' and the dragon who is several times associated with these creatures.

Heorot, too, to which Grendel is distinctly opposed, is partially defined by that opposition. It is a sign of peace and brotherhood, erected by a good ruler as a symbol of good government; Grendel as a sign of fratricide, contention, and social chaos reinforces this basic symbolism of the hall by opposing it. While it is a positive symbol, however, Heorot also connotes the fragility of civilized order both in its vulnerability to Grendel's attacks, the outer sign, and by the presence within it of treasonous men, the moral reality of the sign.

Beowulf's encounter with Grendel's dam may be seen as an extension of his battle with Grendel in defence of Heorot. As has been seen, the Cain tradition associated the first murderer with his mother and made them a pair. Cain was dissociated from his fallen but pious father. The *Beowulf* poet in introducing the female monster emphasizes her sex and the fact of her clan's descent from Cain:

> Þæt hie gesawon swylce twegen
> micle mearcstapan moras healdan,
> ellorgæstas. Ðæra oðer wæs,
> þæs þe hie gewislicost gewitan meahton,
> idese onlicnes. (1347–51)

Earlier on (1258–65) she has been specifically associated, along with her son, with the Cain progeny. The poet deliberately makes ambiguous the patrilineal descent:

> No hie fæder cunnon,
> hwæþer him ænig wæs ær acenned
> dyrnra gasta. (1355–7)

The 'aglaecan' that Beowulf encounters, Unferth's sword in hand, as he approaches Grendel's mother are associated with the monster progeny of Cain alluded to several times before in the poem (1265, for example). The sword is apparently effective against these minor monsters but against Grendel's dam, genetrix of an outlaw race and principle of its continuation, the weapon fails.

The final triumph over the monstrous Cain progeny is the occasion for the important speech known as Hrothgar's 'harangue.' The old warrior who has brought peace to his people, shared his throne with his nephew, and helped to settle foreign feuds now reflects upon the nature of history and moral evil as Beowulf brings to him Grendel's head and the weapon that dealt the final blow in the battle. His moral reflection is prefaced by another allusion to the tradition of cain, for the sword itself is described as 'eotenisc,' giant-wrought, and we recall the medieval legend of the invention of weapons by Cain's descendant, Tubal-Cain, himself a giant and a Vulcan figure, who brought the tools by which bloodshed might be spread in the world. Thus at the moment of Beowulf's greatest victory,

Hrothgar reads upon the hilt of this sword the 'origin of all enmity' and delivers a speech of congratulations and warning. Employing the historical example of Heremod, he cautions the victor against pride and its consequences:

'Wunað he on wiste;   no hine wiht dweleð
adl ne yldo,   ne him inwitsorh
on sefa(n) sweorceð,   ne gesacu ohwær
ecghete eoweð,   ac him eal worold
wendeð on willan;   he þæt wyrse ne con.' (1735–9)

The state here described is that of innocence: on the one hand a general description of every man's innocence before sin; on the other hand a specific reference to the historical figure of the king, Heremod, upon whom God bestowed riches and power to be used in accordance with the law, and who through sin turned the gifts of creation into destruction. Further still, it is a description of the archetypal innocence of Eden and its progressive historical destruction by Cain and his progeny. This is made clearer as Hrothgar continues:

'Oð þæt him on innan   oferhygda dæl
weaxeð ond wridað;   þonne se weard swefeð,
sawele hyrde;   bið se slæp to fæst,
bisgum gebunden,   bona swiðe neah,
se þe of flanbogan   fyrenum sceoteð.
Ðonne bið on hreþre   under helm drepen
biteran stræle   – him bebeorgan ne con – ,
wom wundorbebodum   wergan gastes;
þinceð him to lytel,   þæt he lange heold,
gytsað gromhydig,   nallas on gylp seleð
fætte beagas.' (1740–50)

The victim of sin grows proud, greedy, and niggardly – all vices specifically attributed to the first murderer in the exegetical tradition. He is slowly seduced by his sleeping conscience, and the result is the end of innocence through ambition, greed, and murder; the inspiration of 'wergan gastes.' This is the history of the world as told in Genesis and elaborated in Christian commentary, but equally applicable to the microcosm of the personal moral condition, as in this case that of Heremod. A very similar tropological image had been used to express Cain's moral descent, paralleled by the progressive decadence of civilization. In the fourth century for example, St Basil depicts Cain's moral degeneration in seven steps, chosing that number one supposes, to correspond to the number of generations in Cain's exile:

Now among the daring deeds done by Cain, the first sin is envy at the preference of Abel; the second, guile, whereby he addressed his brother saying: 'Let us go forth into the field'; the third, murder, an added evil; the fourth, that it was even fratricide a greater iniquity; fifth, that Cain was also the first murderer, leaving behind him a bad example for the world; sixth, wrong-doing because he caused grief to his parents; seventh, because he lied to God.[12]

The device of describing Cain's 'psychological' develoment into moral sin was widely used in exegesis. In *Beowulf* we see Hrothgar employ the same device to describe the same moral phenomenon, the passage from innocence to sin. Dramatically the passage functions as a commentary on the significance of the action that has occurred and, of course, as an exhortation to Beowulf. As a commentary on the defeat and destruction of Grendel and his mother, Hrothgar's words are appropriate, for these enemies are the monstrous descendants of the biblical figure who is the origin of the sins enumerated in the harangue. The allusion to Heremod demonstrates, among other things, the continuity of Cain's evil in the post-biblical historic period, and in this sense the speech is one of victory: the defeat of Cain's evil in the destruction of his progeny. It is not possible that the harangue, seen in this way, is delivered by a figure himself guilty of the crimes he deplores. If the poet wished to depict Hrothgar as proud and grasping, he would not put in his mouth the definitive 'explicatio' of the action of the poem up to this point. Such would produce an aesthetic confusion sufficient to dissipate the drama and irony that are otherwise achieved. Hrothgar cannot be a Cain figure celebrating the defeat of other Cain figures. Rather, he seems to be a grateful and wise king who became a victim of the children of Cain because he was so much their antithesis.

Similarly, as an exhortation to Beowulf there is nothing in the speech itself to suggest the ominous irony that the hero will fall prey to the sins of Cain. The dramatic context of the speech would seem to militate against such a view. Beowulf at this moment in the poem is the figure most singularly antithetical to the monsters and their heritage of evil, for he is their nemesis. It is, of course, only in the second part of the poem that the reader sees clearly whether Beowulf has taken Hrothgar's advice, but at the moment of emersion from the mere he is the representative of the force against the evil of Cain.

Beowulf's second battle is the occasion for the poet's description of Grendel's dwelling. Earlier in the poem we are told that the monster dwelt in darkness ('se þe in þystrum bad,' 87), and this feature is repeated frequently.[13] Like Cain, who was always dwelling in darkness, Grendel and his mother inhabit a gloomy region. Cain, having polluted the earth with human and sibling blood, was banished into a place of infertility, a waste inhabited only by beasts, of whom he had become one. Thus St Ambrose describes Cain's exile abode as one in which his ways become bestial.[14] So, too, is Grendel's home: 'fen ond fæsten; fifelcynnes eard' (104). A dweller in swamps and fens and moors, Grendel has found the Danish equivalent to the wasteland of his forefather. The poet is specific in relating that Grendel has been exiled to such a place because of Cain's fratricide, and this statement is reinforced by the depiction of Grendel's abode in terms used by exegetes to describe Cain's dwelling.

The same dwelling is further described when the poet speaks of Grendel's dam:

Ides aglæcwif   yrmþe gemunde,
se þe wæteregesan   wunian scolde,
cealde streamas,   siþðan Cain wearð
to ecgbanan   angan breþer. (1259–62)

And further on:

'Hie dygel lond
warigeað wulfhleoþu,   windige næssas,
frecne fengelad,   ðær fyrgenstream
under næssa genipu   niþer gewiteð.' (1357–60)

Beowulf seeks the monster's home underwater and underground at the bottom of a lake:

Ða se earl ongeat,
þæt he[in] niðsele   nathwylcum wæs,
þær him nænig wæter   wihte ne sceþede. (1512–14)

Here one may recall that according to Jewish tradition the descendants of Cain had dwellings underwater similar to his, and in the *Midrash Konen*, for example, one finds the tradition that Cain's offspring lived underground.[15]

The locus of the monsters would seem, then, related to the tradition of Nod[16] and the wild place of exile of Cain's brood. Within the tradition, too, would seem to be the poet's description of the rise of the race of monsters on earth:

Þanon untydras   ealle onwocon,
eotenas ond ylfe   ond orcneas,
swylce gigantas,   þa wið Gode wunnon
lange þrage;   he him ðæs lean forgeald. (111–14)

And later:

Þanon woc fela
geosceaftgasta;   wæs þæra Grendel sum,
heorowearh hetelic. (1265–7)

The earlier passage reads not unlike a brief encyclopaedia of the monstrous race, a selection from the *Liber Monstrorum*. Cannibal giants ('eotenas'), incubus-like spirits ('ylfe'), water beasts ('orcneas'), and giants are part of the clan to which Cain belongs, and all are sired by Cain.

The presence of the monster's mother within the poem also suggests the tradition. Augustine, as we have seen, discusses the idea that had grown up among the literal-minded that since no other woman was available, Cain took his own mother, Eve, as wife and went into Nod with her. Thus the association of Eve and Cain as an unholy incestuous pair existed in popular legend and may well have had some influence on the presence of Grendel's mother in the poem. The middle ages popularly conceived of evil as having initially been spread in the world by this pair, Eve and her wicked son, who were not only incestuous but who each in his own way had caused man's progressive fall. The dramatic purpose of Grendel's mother in the poem is to present a certain order within the monstrous, an inverted kin, which tends to mirror and emphasize the idea of order particularized as kinship within the historical societies and figures of the poem. Beowulf, who above all values kinship, is thus the contradiction of the clan whose negation of this value welds its members together into an anti-kin. Nevertheless, in the poem the monsters are given a careful pedigree: Grendel is a kinsman, and we encounter with Beowulf another of his kin. Together this kin belongs to a larger clan, the 'eotens,' giants and spirits who dwell around the melancholy mere. And further, this clan has a genealogy stretching back through Goliath, Ham, and Cain to the beginning of time. Thus it becomes a nightmare version of society and civilization with its own inverted order and social system.

Vengeance, a primary value in Germanic society, is immediately undertaken by Grendel's mother with the injury to her son, demonstrating that in her kin, too, it is a value. With this touch the poet provides through analogy a subtle comment on the worthiness of the values of pagan society, a subject he develops more directly in the 'digressions.' At this point, however, we notice one of the skilful ways in which the fabulous world of Grendel interlocks with the historical world of the Danes and provides an implicit didactic comment on it.

Hrothgar's society is a historical phenomenon existing in a particular point in time and space. The first menace to it that we see resolved in Beowulf's two battles with the monsters is of another order, although manifesting itself in time and space, for it is the eternal spirit of bloodshed and war embodied in the monster and related to an uninterrupted force of evil beginning with Cain. In this sense the battle with the monsters is appropriately rendered fabulous, for it is of another order and greater significance than other battles. The rhetorical description of the battle at Ravenswood, for instance, is distinctly different from that of the battle with Grendel or the battle with his dam. The setting of the former is ordinary and identifiable, and can be said to be undistinguished as a place. The scene of Grendel's cave, on the other hand, is eerie and fantastic. The battle of Ravenswood is fought through conventional military tactics with everyday weapons. Beowulf's underwater victory is marked by divine intercession and magic weapons. In the one case the opponents are ordinary characters of history; in the other, monsters and a superhuman hero.

The fabulous characteristics are easily perceived in both the fight with Grendel and the fight with the dragon. They are the presence of monsters, wondrous weapons, and supernatural strength. The function of the fabulous within the poem would seem to be to express the transtemporal nature of the meaning of the conflict that takes place in that mode. The fabulous battles, while happening in time and place and being full of blood, bring to the foreground the fundamental conflict between the forces of disorder and the forces of order, the forces of hate and the forces of love, the one rendered in monstrous form associated with the Cain tradition, the other in heroic form and associated with the heroes of good throughout history.

There are, to be sure, more particular expressions of the same conflict, but these are specified in the poem as historic incidents. One such would be the fight at Finnsburg. In these manifestations the opponents are mundane, the motive for the action involves personal gain, and the significance of the event is thus somewhat circumscribed. The function of the fabulous, then, is to broaden the significance of these historic events and to provide for them a tropologial context through which this meaning can be seen. In the fabulous mode of the poem we learn that enmity and bloodshed are present in the world through Cain's spirit of vengeance and fratricide. Because of this we are permitted to see the pattern in the relationship of the many historic incidents in the poem that, limited as they are by temporal constraints, we might otherwise not perceive. In every case the bridge from the fabulous to the historic is Beowulf himself. It is remarkable that despite the opportunities in the plot of the poem we never are allowed to see Beowulf in battle with historical figures, only with the monsters. Yet this hero of the fabulous is the means by which every historical incident, past and future, is introduced: the story of Sigemund is told to introduce a positive comparison to him; that of Heremod, in order to show his opposite; the story of Freawaru is his own prophecy; Wealhtheow's plea, a dramatic allusion to the future, is directed to him.

The full analysis of the historic incidents will be offered in the next section, but so closely related are the fabulous and historic in the poem that it is difficult to discuss one without reference to the other. Beowulf, himself both fabulous and historic, engages the monsters in Denmark in a battle that we can call fabulous in the sense just described. Once home in Geatland, he is again enjoined in battle of a fabulous nature in which the poet completes the expression of the theme in that mode and provides the full context in which the historic events, and history itself, can be understood.

The other historic kingdom presented to us in the present time of the poem is that of Geatland. The parallels between the two halves of the poem are several and fundamental. As in the case of Denmark, Beowulf's Geatland is presented as a peaceful and harmonious society:

> 'Næs se folccyning,
> ymbesittendra   ænig ðara,

þe mec guðwinum   gretan dorste,
egesan ðeon.' (2733–6)

Like Denmark, Geatland is attacked by a monster whose ravishes, although committed for different motives, have a similarly devastating effect on the society. Again as in Denmark, Beowulf – here both monster fighter and king – rids the society of the monstrous menace, although, not unlike the allusions to Danish future, references to Geatish future suggest catastrophe after Beowulf's departure.

The peace and kin respect inaugurated in Beowulf's reign contrast with the immediate past of Geatland, as did Hrothgar's reign with the past of Denmark. Both the history of the house of Hrethel and the circumstances of Hygelac's own demise contain the themes familiar to all major incidents of the poem, those of parricide and war.

Hygelac's death is the result of his having become overwhelmed by pride and greed and having created enmity and feud with the Franks. The poet states this clearly and directly:

Hyne wyrd fornam,
syþðan he for wlenco   wean ahsode,
fæhðe to Frysum.   He þa frætwe wæg,
eorclanstanas   ofer yða ful. (1205–8)

Thus the motive for the war against his southern neighbours is simply that of lust, as far as the poem tells us. The vehicle for the story of the raid is the allusion to the necklace given in tribute to Beowulf after his victory in Denmark. Hygelac wore the necklace, we are told, when he plundered the Franks. The poet uses this allusion as the occasion for further allusion to the 'Brosinga' jewel and intimately associates the two. Thus the fall of Hygelac becomes the occasion for the telling of the story of Eormanric and the 'Brosinga mene.'

The entire matter of the Eormanric-Harlung story is a confusing one, but certain features of it that are known may possibly be related to the Geat King's death. From legend and history[17] we know that Eormanric was an early king of the Goths. His nephews, the Harlungs, are shadowy figures of myth and folklore. They dwelt near Breisach in the area of the Black Forest, it is supposed, and possessed an immense treasure, the pride of which was the Brosing necklace. The story, pieced together from German and Scandinavian literature, describes them as having been murdered by their uncle Eormanric and robbed of the necklace. The bloodthirsty nature of Eormanric is fully borne out by the rest of the story surrounding him, the most famous event of which is his murder of his wife, Swanhild, and of his son. This legendary parricide – slayer of son, nephews, and wife – is the figure most closely associated with the jewel.

Like parts of a fan, a series of allusions opens out to suggest associated themes: Beowulf's necklace symbol of triumpth over blood-lust; Hygelac's raid, inspired by greed and pride; the 'Brosinga mene,' token of parricide and greed; and Hygelac's death and loss of Beowulf's necklace to his enemies. It is a panorama not unfamiliar to the audience of this poem.

Hygelac's death is the occasion for the ascension of his son, Heardred, to the throne. The subsequent death of the young king and part of the story of Swedish enmity are interrelated and seem to form a single episode presented in the poetic present of *Beowulf*. Other episodes in this enmity are presented as allusions to the historic past.

The history leading to Onela's kinship in Sweden is vague, and the text of the poem gives little help in clarifying it. We know that bad relations existed between Onela and his nephews, Eanmund and Eadgils, sons of the former king, and it is likely that possession of the throne is at the centre of the dispute. Thus, as in so many incidents of Germanic history, the morally sacred relation of uncle-nephew is corrupted by ambition, although in the present case by whose ambition it is unclear. At any rate, upon Onela's succession to the throne the nephews rebel and are pursued into Geatland, whereupon the Swedish episode becomes involved in the death of Heardred:

> Hyne wræcmæcgas
> ofer sæ sohtan,   suna Ohteres;
> hæfdon hy forhealden   helm Scylfinga,
> þone selestan   sæcyninga
> þara ðe in Swiorice   sinc brytnade,
> mærne þeoden.   Him þæt to mearce wearð;
> he þære [f]or feorme   feorhwunde hleat,
> sweordes swengum,   sunu Hygelaces. (2379–86)

Onela's attack upon the Geats is partially successful since he achieves the death of one of his nephews and that of their protector through the agency of Weohstan, as the poem specifies:

> þæt wæs mid eldum   Eanmundes laf,
> suna Ohtere[s];   þam æt sæcce wearð,

wræcca(n) wineleasum Weohstan bana
meces ecgum, ond his magum ætbær
brunfagne helm, hringde byrnan,
ealdsweord etonisc; þæt him Onela forgeaf,
his gædelinges guðgewædu,
fyrdsearo fuslic, – no ymbe ða fæhðe spræc,
þeah ðe he his broðor bearn abredwade. (2611–19)

We have, then, as the background to Heardred's fall a tale of parricide and vengeance, the Cain-inspired crime that Beowulf battled in monster form in Denmark.

The question of guilt in this episode remains, however, an enigmatic one. On the one hand, the poet's ironic emphasis on Onela's ability to forgive the slaying of a kinsman (2616–19) seems to suggest the uncle's malevolence. Beowulf's later campaign against him would tend to strengthen this suggestion and place Onela among the forces of Cain combatted by the hero throughout the poem. Over against this we have the poet's description of him as 'selestan sæcyninga' (2382), and no reference to his possessing the throne illegally.

Eanmund and Eadgils are described as 'wræcmæcgas' (2379), 'exiles,' which, if they are seen as the guilty ones, may have been a penalty, like Cain's, for a particularly antisocial crime. Eadgil's character and later role in the destruction of the Geats can be seen to support a theory of his malice in the incident. It is not, however essential to place guilt. What is noteworthy is that the contemporary history of Geatland, the fall of Heardred, and the context of Beowulf's ascension to the throne are presented through a historical theme of kin violation and Cain-inspired violence. Thus Beowulf, who has fought a Cain-descended monster in Denmark and who will, as guardian of social good, fight another peace-hating monster in Geatland, is made king through the effects of a historical act the moral quality of which would have been associated with the spirit of Cain.

Further, the Swedish situation is not unlike the Danish one alluded to earlier in the poem in which a nephew, Hrothulf, apparently resentfully awaits his chance to slay uncle and cousins alike in his desire for the throne. Contrasting with both these situations are Beowulf's relationship to Hygelac, an ideal kinship bond free of the taint of ambition, and later his relationship to Heardred, which begins when he turns down an offer of the throne in order to respect natural heritage. Beowulf even acts as tutor to the weak and inexperienced king. Both of these relationships, each of which reflects in a sense the degree of stability of Geatish society, are destroyed through the death of one of the partners in circumstances echoing the Cain theme of the 'fabulous' level of the poem.

Thus the concern in the poem with the fragility of civilization and man's social institutions is not purely an abstract one figured forth in struggles with grotesque beasts. The poet presents here, and, as we will see in the next section, through all the historic allusions past and future, an example of a society threatened by internecine wars and the human vices of greed, ambition, bloodthirstiness, and kin hate. The future entanglement of incidents and characters in this Swedish episode with the future and the fate of Beowulf's society, which will be discussed in the next section, illustrates even more clearly the poet's vision of the role of the children of Cain in history and his image of the man transformed into monster through his imitation of Cain. It is in such a historical context that Beowulf meets the dragon.

The third foe that Beowulf meets is perhaps the most complicated and symbolically rich monster in the whole medieval tradition of teratology. Considering only his European manifestations, although he is of all monsters truly universal, the dragon is a constant actor in the symbolic drama of developing human consciousness. Several characteristics are invariable. His dwelling is regularly underground or underwater, and he usually attacks a citadel. The destruction of the dragon leads to the salvation of the city. Thus the story of the dragon slain by Cadmus may be seen as an embryonic expression of the tension between dragon and city, for the dragon's role is to prevent the founding of Thebes and the consequent inauguration of a new age of civilization. From his teeth are born those who will eventually destroy Thebes. In the many versions of the story of St George, the dragon holds hostage a city from which inhabitants are sent to be his food. The dragon, then, is seen as the particular force that negates civilization. He is an underground creature signifying passion and chaos and detesting reason and order as symbolized by the city and by light and upon which civilization is based.

In the middle ages the dragon also symbolized death in his underground aspect, in contrast again to the city as an image of life and social intercourse. Before and after the middle ages he was a figure for time as related to death in time's aspect of consummation and destruction. Civilization with its institutions dedicated to law, propagation, and social development by its very nature wages war on this facet of time and poses against it the phenomenon of continuity. Thus the underground serpent, like the underground Grendel, is the figure of antithesis of the above-ground city and its institutions based on the light of reason.

The other regular feature of the dragon is his treasure. Indeed, his underground home accounts for his possession of gold and gems, since they are products of the womb of the earth. While the treasure itself is neither good nor bad, the dragon's possession of it is evil, for the treasure symbolizes knowledge and challenge: 'Ce trésor gardé n'est pas toujours un tas d'or que convoite l'avaricieux, et la gemme n'est pas non plus seulement une pierre précieuse facile a monnayer. Ce sont aussi et sourtout des images de la connaissance et de la difficulté surmontée.'[18] Similarly, we read in Ecclesiastes 20:32 'Wisdom that is hid, and treasure that is not seen, what profit is there in them both.'

Every culture attributes mythical and magical properties to ore and gems besides adorning the invention of such elements and their exploitation with legends. Most cultures, as well, associate the dragon with these subterranean properties. The Christian legends, some of which we have seen already, attributed the mining of metals and gems from the earth to the depravity of demons who instructed early man in the magic needed to use these elements. More specifically, the angels who had lusted after the daughters of Cain were so seduced by these women that they revealed to them the magical arts concerning gems and metals. Soon after, Tubal-Cain, one of the three archetypal descendants of Cain, relied on this knowledge of metal to invent the art of weaponry. When God took offence at the evil development of man and washed away civilization with the Flood, Ham, won over by the giants who were considered the guardians of the evil knowledge, inscribed the magic formulae of the art on stones, and in that way the use of ore and gems was perpetuated. The dragon, then, seen in medieval tradition as the guardian of buried treasure, performs a function analogous to that of Cain-descended giants in pre-diluvian society in preventing man from using metal and gems representing knowledge.

In Christian tradition the treasure is nevertheless dubious. In one sense it represents the unhappy complication of innocent society, entailing as it does the use of metal as money, weapons, and weights. In a similar way Eve's acquisitive desire for knowledge was seen as tragic. Once the treasure is revealed, however, man falls under the obligation to use it piously and wisely.[19] Thus jewels were regularly used to decorate icons and metals to build machines for the progess of civilization in the middle ages. Similarly, human knowledge beginning in Eden, while considered inferior to the state of innocence that preceded it, was nevertheless seen in medieval theology as the necessary means to the recapturing of the lost state.

The dragon, then, is twice condemned. He is, of course, a form of Satan, and as associated with the treasures of the earth's entrails he is regarded as introducing into the world a corrupting influence. Secondly, in further preventing the conversion of the treasure to redemptive purposes by hoarding it, he is considered an enemy of progress and knowledge. The dragon is a Vulcan–Tubal-Cain figure embodying the most potent of antisocial forces whose destruction is the challenge that must be met by all heroes in order to possess his treasure, the knowledge of the nature of things.

Neither in *Beowulf* nor in exegesis is the dragon identified as a descendant of Cain, but in both there is a relation of the two in their similar habits. As seen above, the dragon performs a function similar to that of the other children of Cain in relation to the secrets of the earth. In *Beowulf* the dragon's chief role seems to be as an enemy of peace and of ordered society. Exegesis normally interpreted the dragon as a form of demon or Satan himself, just as it interpreted Cain as a manifestation of the Devil. In the poem Beowulf is described as having passed his youth battling 'untydras' that continue the satanic influence. The reinforcement of Beowulf as hero in opposition to this evil continues on several levels at once. In battle Beowulf is the physical destroyer of the monsters that bring feud and social chaos upon men; as retainer and kinsman he is the moral force that resists the bloodthirsty jealousy of Cain and upholds the values of brotherhood and fidelity; and as king he is the historical force of peace and harmony in a long history of vengeance and regicide that holds at bay the revenge of his enemies who have followed in the way of Cain and Heremod. Just as the model society that Hrothgar established in Heorot was menaced by a monster, so the ideal reign of Beowulf is marred by the attacks of another monster:

> Oð ðæt an ongan
> deorcum nihtum   draca rics[i] an,
> se ðe on hea(um) h(æþ)e   hord beweotode. (2210–12)

There is something familiar about this new monster in the poem, and his introduction does not seem altogether unprepared for. When Beowulf visits the exile abode of Grendel, the waste so like that of Nod, he meets there other creatures that share the company of Grendel and his mother, and he beholds the kin of the Cain-descended sinner: 'wyrmcynnes fela'

(1435), 'sædracan' (1426), 'wyrmas' (1430). When he has completed his victory over Cain's agent, his triumph is compared with that of Sigemund, who fought not a troll but a dragon: 'wyrm acwealde' (886). It would seem, then, that the monster Beowulf meets in Geatland is not something unknown to him or utterly different in physical form from the monsters he has already fought, and is quite similar in the evil it represents.

Beowulf himself associates the dragon with Grendel and his dam, and we perceive that as Grendel represented the persistence of the spirit of Cain in its particular harassment of the Danish court, so the dragon draws his significance from his action in destroying the peace and harmony of Geatish society; he is the counterpart of Hrothgar's nemesis. Beowulf thinks immediately of his previous contest with Grendel as he faces the dragon:

'Nolde ic sweord beran,
wæpen to wyrme,   gif ic wiste hu
wið ðam aglæcean   elles meahte
gylpe wiðgripan,   swa ic gio wið Grendle dyde.' (2518–21)

The poet's choice of vocabulary for the description of the dragaon also suggests his conception of the monster's nature. The dragon is variously called 'uhtsceaða' (2271), 'mansceaða' (2514), 'ðeodsceaða' (2278, 2688). It is interesting that Grendel has been generally described in similar ways as 'dolsceaða' (479), 'manscaða' (712, 737), and 'leodsceaða' (2093). They are both described generally as 'feond' and more particularly designated as demons, 'gæst' (102, 2312), 'ellengæst' (86), 'wælgæst' (1995). The dragon is 'gryregieste' (2560), and Grendel sings a 'gryreleod' (786); the troll does 'niþgeweorca' (683) and 'nydwracu niþgrim' (193), while the dragon is a 'niþgæst' (2699) and 'niþdraca' (2273). Beowulf arms himself against the 'inwitfeng' (1447) of monsters in the fight with Grendel's dam and later arms himself against the 'inwitgæst' (2670) in the dragon contest.

Whatever value such corraborative evidence may have in indicating the poet's intention to relate the dragon to the idea of Cain, the ultimate demonstration of that proposition rests upon the thematic function of the dragon. If the contest has any significance beyond an adventure story – and all other signs indicate that it does – it may be in the dragon's relationship to Grendel and the other figures in the medieval tradition of monsters that such significance is to be perceived. Structurally the poem demands a relationship between the monsters, for the two episodes concerning them are essential balances in a structure of balance: as has been so often noted, the first part of the poem takes place in a ravaged court of Denmark, the second in the ravaged court of Geats; Beowulf's first contest is with a Cain-descended monster, his second with another monster threatening social order.

In theme, also, the dragon battle complements and continues the fight with Grendel. Beowulf's reign, like Hrothgar's, has been a golden age of peace. It has seen the end of foreign enmities and domestic unrest, and it is upon this ideal state that the dragon bursts, at night like Grendel, with his destructive wrath. As we know, the dragon's evil will result in the death of Beowulf, and not only the death of the king but ultimately, as Wiglaf predicts, the destruction of Geatish civilization.

The poet tells us that the dragon has long held the treasure unjustly and, what is more, that he who hid it was also guilty of wrongdoing (3059). There is here an allusion to the evil of hiding and hoarding treasure. It is referred to as 'hæðnum horde' (2216), and its monstrous guardian is seen as dedicated to exactly the same end as the heathens who hid it in the first place: to prevent other men and society from profiting by it.

The symbolic significance of treasure and its possession cannot be overlooked in attempting to analyse the meaning of the dragon episode in *Beowulf*. Such a consideration would lead one to disagree with Goldsmith's claim that the treasure was part of the 'temporalia' to which the hero had become sinfully attached, for this may be to take a too pecuniary attitude towards the treasure. As Michael Cherniss has pointed out, modern critics have misunderstood the role of treasure in accusing Beowulf of avarice,[20] and he reminds us of Dorothy Whitelock's earlier demonstration that the function of treasure is to enhance and enlarge the image of the possessor.[21] More recently, John Gardner has pointed out the clearly positive function of treasure in *Daniel*: 'The first of the controlling ideas in "Daniel" is stock in Old English biblical verse translation: obedience to God wins characteristically Teutonic tribal wealth and strength: "goldhord" and "cyningdom".'[22]

Among the highest values in Anglo-Saxon society, as we know, was that of sharing or ring giving. The ceremonial distribution of treasure expressed the nature of civilization itself in that it was a form of communication, a sign of essential bonds existing between men that formed the corner-stone of civilization itself. We may recall that one of the original sins of Cain was niggardliness, and this vice was constantly associated with his race and with all antisocial behavior. Hoarding, then, suggests the opposite of this social value of sharing, as does the solitary state of the hoarder, not unlike the state of exile also associated with Cain and his race.

The treasure may be seen in both its literal and metaphoric senses. In the first sense it is a resource for a peaceful society at a high point in its development as a civilization; and the poem seems to suggest that the thief had just such a practical motive for his action. As symbol, the treasure may be seen in two ways. First, it is a fitting image for a society in its golden age; as the Danes built Heorot at such a point in their development, so the Geats might have used the great treasure as an image of their own greatness. Further, hidden treasure, at least when guarded by a dragon, is the symbol of wisdom as yet unattained and a challenge as yet unmet. Since Beowulf has brought stability to his country, subdued its enemies, and established a very long reign of peace, his possession of the treasure to signify a challenge met would be appropriate, for as the poem so sadly demonstrates, the greatest challenge to any king of the time was the achievement of peace. And as we see in his 'apologia' before battle, Beowulf has also achieved a state of wisdom not inferior to Hrothgar's: a wisdom concerning the nature of evil, the vulnerability of society, and the significance of history. The reburial of the treasure after his death, far from corroborating Beowulf's guilt in having possessed it, would seem to connote the end of his achievement and the Geats' loss of his moral-historical understanding.

The serf or thane (the manuscript is corrupt) who breaks into the dragon's hoard can hardly be regarded as an evil man, considering both the poet's statements and the nature of those whom the thief offends. If it is wrong to hide treasure, and if the dragon is evil to hold it, it is difficult to regard the thief as the protagonist of evil. Indeed, the poet depicts him as especially favoured by God:

> Swa mæg unfæge   eaðe gedigan
> wean ond wræcsið   se ðe Waldendes
> hyldo gehealdeþ! (2291–3)

Further, we know that the purpose of the theft was to gain enough gold to pay wergeld and avoid feud and bloodshed. In many more important instances the poet omits to give us reasons for the actions of his characters, yet here in the case of a relatively insignificant character he has taken some pains to assign a motive for the theft of the cup:

> Nealles mid gewealdum   wyrmhord abræc,
> sylfes willum,   se ðe him sare gesceod,
> ac for þreanedlan   þ(eow)[23] nathwylces
> hæleða bearna   heteswengeas fleah. (2221–4)

As a clarification of the thief's motive the passage also helps to indicate the possible motives of the dragon. It will be recalled that Grendel is particularly condemned for his refusal to settle his feud by wergeld, and an echo of his refusal seems to exist in the dragon's opposition to the use of his treasure for peaceful settlements. The thief brought the cup to his lord – apparently Beowulf, since the cup is next seen in his possession – an action that according to W.W. Lawrence involves Beowulf in the attempt at peaceful settlement: 'Similarly, in the final adventure of the poem, the hoard of the dragon was plundered by a man who wished to get treasure to buy off an injury, and Beowulf, then king of the Geatas, apparently acted as mediator in the affair.'[24] The suitability of a gold cup for such a purpose is suggested in Frederic Seebohm's description of the method of payment of wergeld and fines in Anglo-Saxon law: 'There is plenty of evidence to show that large payments of gold and silver were mostly made by weight, and very often in gold articles.'[25]

The dragon's significance seems to be first in his opposition to this attempt at peaceful settlement whereby he reveals his similarity to Cain and his race as a promoter of violence and feud. As wergeld was the only means, albeit finally an inadequate one, by which primitive society might avoid violent retribution and social chaos, the dragon's second and more general significance is as an enemy of civilization itself, a role consonant with the universal symbolism of the dragon and one linking him even more intimately with the spirit of Cain in the poem. We know, as did the audience of *Beowulf*, that vengeance will indeed be taken if wergeld is not paid; that is how a bloody feud began, and it is a feud that will eventually rend asunder the civilization of the Geats. The use of the dragon in this way, then, is a highly dramatic stroke in the poem and one that recalls the use of Grendel's ravages as a paradigm for the historic destruction of Heorot. The dragon is vengeance and enmity embodied in a fabulous beast. He hides treasure that could be used as a means of social good, as the pagans in *Elene* hide the true cross – not for their own good, but to deprive men of its benefits.

In the cases of both Grendel and the dragon, motivation for their destructive rage is found within the mere fact and potential for peace. Grendel hears sounds of brotherhood within Heorot and attacks. The dragon loses a gold cup in the name of peaceful settlement and begins to devastate the kingdom, and Cain, according to St Augustine, was inspired to fratricide by the simple spectacle of goodness.[26] For the second time it is Beowulf who opposes such monstrous evil and asserts himself as the contrasting force of good. The death of Beowulf is the final comment on the virulence of this evil and the way of the world, this force of Cain 'which is ever dying, and never dead.'[27]

Such a theme would seem to be reinforced by the poet's inclusion of the struggle with Grendel's dam among Beowulf's feats. Her renewal of the attack on Heorot emphasizes the malignancy and strength of her clan's power, and it is with utter discouragement that the Danes witness the female monster's destruction. The poetic effect of this recurrence is to underscore the persistence of the evil that menaces the Danes, the ineradicability of bloodthirstiness. With the destruction of Grendel's dam the Danes are henceforth free from the threat in monstrous form, as far as the narrative tells us; it is as if in the obliteration of the female of this clan, whose power includes generation, one branch of Cain's progeny is truly destroyed. But the later appearance of the dragon as a representative of violence and blood-lust would seem to recall in a particular way the constancy of the antisocial force in human society and prepare us to look for its other manifestations in such different modes as human Cain figures in history. Thus, although the dragon, like Grendel and his dam, is physically destroyed in combat with Beowulf, immediate reference is made to the future expression of the same force by the historic enemies of the Geats.

One must pause here to take issue with a particular element of Goldsmith's thesis that sees the poem as depicting the hero's unsuccessful struggle with the Devil. In order to invest the allegory of the poem with a formality and consistency probably foreign to it, Goldsmith finds it necessary to regard Beowulf's defeat by the dragon as a token of the hero's guilt in having become too attached to the things of the world: 'The unease that he [Beowulf] felt seems more probably the realization that he had become content to enjoy the "temporalia" that were his in abundance, and, as Hrothgar had foretold, had neglected the service of his Lord.'[28] The first thing to note here is that Hrothgar in no way 'foretold' such an event, but instead warned against it. The difference between a prophecy and an exhortation is both rhetorically formal and of great thematic importance. Further, it would be in marked contrast to Beowulf's character as witnessed in his refusal of Hygd's offer of the throne on ethical grounds to become suddenly covetous of the benefits of power in later life. It is, of course, aesthetically possible to have managed the poem that way, but the audience would certainly expect and require clear signs of such a shift in moral disposition. The text does not seem to provide such signs and in fact may be seen to provide indications of a quite opposite nature. Nowhere do we see Beowulf described as guilty of cupidity, much less abandoning the service of God. Rather, in Beowulf's 'apology' we see both an account of his actions on earth and an expression of the moral basis for them. But

Goldsmith feels that the declaration of avoiding the major evils of the time is insufficient: 'As the climax of the list of evil acts eschewed he [Beowulf] puts the murder of kinsmen ... Kaske says that this speech "illustrates his *sapientia* by his avoidance of the major forms of Germanic wrongdoing (2736–43), all of them Christian sins as well". If so, it is a curiously limited sort of *sapientia*.'[29]

It must be observed, however, that love of peace is not a lesser virtue, although it may not be accurate to call it *sapientia*. This is especially true in the context of a poem the theme of which is the constant negation of peace throughout history. The poetic requirements (the moral requirements are not primary) are that in the last moments of his life and at the close of the poem a clear statement of what the hero represents must be provided. The context in which this requirement arises is that of a poem describing the hero's struggle with two peace-destroying monsters – one descended from Cain and suggesting fratricide, the other a form of Satan and suggesting blood feud – extended and developed by a number of historical allusions each of which bears a theme of fratricide and vengeance, or their opposites. The statement that the poet provides seems admirably straightforward; the hero represents peace ('ne sohte searoniðas,' 2738), righteousness ('ne me swor fela / aða on unriht,' 2738–9) and brotherhood ('me witan ne ðearf Waldend fira / morðorbealo maga,' 2741–2), and he has provided a long and stable government in a time of menace (2732–3).

Goldsmith's claim that 'Beowulf's zeal for fame quite evidently proved calamitous to his people'[30] certainly seems to change the force of the text. It was not Beowulf's desire for fame that proved calamitous to the Geats, but rather his death! It is fairly clear that Beowulf had, for a Germanic ruler, a rather unusual lack of desire for fame, or else why did he waste fifty years keeping peace instead of pursuing glorious battle? It is instead the very fact of Beowulf's mortality that condemns the Geats and provides a final, ironic comment on the nature of social life and man's moral struggle. Every man must die, even the hero, and after his death the forces of evil kept at bay by his strength may overcome the civilization protected by him. Such would seem to be the *Beowulf* poet's message in his skilful management of the figure of Wiglaf as the explanation of the fate of the Geats. Thus, on the contrary, only Beowulf and his virtue prevented the social calamity that awaited his people. Upon his death the inevitable occurred. The fall of the Geats, like the fall of so many nations, would seem to be suggested as inevitable in the poem because of the inability of pagan social institutions to guarantee peace and order.

One can, however, agree with Goldsmith's suggestion that the dragon episode is meant to suggest the Grendel episode and that the dragon functions generally as 'the Ancient Serpent, whose sins, like Adam's, are "oferhydo and gifernesse." '[31] It is also suggested, perhaps, that it is from his experience with the dragon that Beowulf learns how feud and enmity are born among men, the social predicament, as Hrothgar had learned years before from the hilt of a sword the nature of this evil's continuity, the historical predicament. Thus the wisdom symbolized by the treasure that Beowulf wins would seem to be in his final perception of the tragedy of man's social predicament: 'Hæfde þa gefrunen, hwanan sio fæhð aras, / bealoni∂ biorna' (2403–4). We may find here an echo of the description of Hrothgar's perception of the nature of evil:

> Hylt sceawode,
> ealde lafe, on ∂æm wæs or writen
> fyrngewinnes, syðþan flod ofsloh,
> gifen geotende giganta cyn. (1687–90)

Beowulf is at this point an old king who in his youth had battled monsters and throughout his career continued his opposition to their evil in all its manifestations. There is no specific indication in the poem that Beowulf at any given point before meeting the dragon fully understands the nature of the evil he opposes; otherwise he might not have misplaced his trust in Unferth. It would seem that now, at the end of his life with the means of peaceful settlement in his hands, Beowulf comprehends something of the significance of social evil in its moral and historical dimensions and perceives, perhaps, the fatal weakness of his civilization.

Beowulf may at this point, as he prepares to do battle with another agent of destruction, realize that the evil of blood-lust that he fought in the form of Grendel was not one confined to grotesques and monsters or limited to haphazard occurrence, but a force that belongs to an ancient and persistent tradition possessing its own historical continuity and which is basic to human society itself; a tradition that has as its goal the destruction of order and civilization. Beowulf may also perceive that this order has as its agents not only the historical offspring of Cain but his spiritual heirs, as well, among men of every age, for straightaway he launches into a description of a central historical incident of fratricide in the Geatish royal house:

> 'Wæs þam yldestan ungedefelice
> mæges dædum morþorbed stred,
> syððan hyne Hæðcyn of hornbogan,
> his freawine flane geswencte.' (2435–8)

The further relation of the dragon to the Cain tradition can be seen in some of the more minor elements of the legend. The exegets described among the sins of Cain and his descendants the impiety of having constructed cities, the first erected by mankind. Principally the cities of Enoch and Babylon were symbols of outrage to the Lord, the former being Cain's own attempt to defy his punishment of exile. The latter is the symbol of the survival of Cain's giant progeny and their enormous sacrilege. The denotation of cities in Anglo-Saxon literature as 'giants' work' is widespread, and bearing in mind the same description in Scripture and exegesis, it is interesting to find the dragon of *Beowulf* inhabiting what seems to be the ruins of a city built by giants,[32] or a burial vault:

> Seah on enta geweorc
> hu ða stanbogan   stapulum fæste
> ece eorðreced   innan healde. (2717–19)

Likewise the treasure guarded within this place by the dragon is called the work of giants:

> 'Ða ic on hlæwe gefrægn   hord reafian,
> eald enta geweorc   anne mannan.' (2773–4)

Treasure, consisting as it does of jewels and ore when it is described as having been made or worked, probably refers to objects made of metal and decorated with jewels and thus may here contain an echo of the tradition that connected the Vulcan–Tubal-Cain myth to the mysteries of the bowels of the earth.

Particularly disastrous from the social point of view was the invention of weapons. The sword as the chief weapon in war was seen as marking a particular step in the degeneration of human society. As the sword was the invention of Tubal-Cain and the giants, the designation of a weapon as 'giant-made sword' was probably meant to evoke an entire history of social decadence beginning with Babel and continuing through the Flood until the historical present.

In Beowulf's battle with Grendel's clan his sword fails him, just as it does in his fight with the dragon. It would seem that in battle with certain monsters, weapons that match the enemies' extraordinary power are required. Grendel's dam is defeated with a sword described in wondrous terms and designated 'giant-made.' The 'ealdsweord eotenisc' (1558) with which Beowulf saves his life is also called 'giganta geweorc' (1562) and is later inextricably related to Cain tradition when upon its hilt are discovered runes relating the story of the Flood and its causes. There is in Germanic literature the tradition of the wonder smith, the special might of ancient weapons, and the whole story of Wieland. There is also the scriptural tradition of the origin of weapons, which one imagines a Christian poet would hardly ignore, especially in a composition full of references to Cain. Germanic tradition does not account for specifically giant-made swords, but Christian tradition does. In Christian tradition, as well, the double significance of such swords as good and evil may be found. As has been indicated earlier, Christian allegory complemented the sword of enmity of Tubal-Cain with the sword of justice, and thus an 'old giant sword' may be wielded in a right cause or a wrong one.

What is significant in all this in relation to the dragon is that this monster, too, cannot be killed by ordinary weapons but succumbs when struck by an 'ealdsweord eotenisc' (2616). The dragon is in this way related to the earlier monster that Beowulf has slain since both are seen to possess a virulence matched only by the virulence of a monster-wrought weapon. It is principally in the dragon's prevention of peaceful settlement that we see his significance, but a whole web of interrelations and allusions to the unbroken tradition of antisocial evil augment and focus this central revelation.

The interrelation of the fabulous and historic in the poetic present has been seen in the two geographical loci of Denmark and Geatland. In the main action of the poem taking place in present time, Beowulf and Hrothgar as historical figures, as well as several historical characters related to them, are seen in opposition to the fabulous monsters representative of the spirit of Cain. This contrasting pair of modes, historic and fabulous, would seem to be related to an alternate mode in the poem, often called 'the digressions,' which we may here call the past through allusion and the future through prophecy. The nature of the relationship of the historic-fabulous to the future-past modes would seem to be that the former creates a paradigm for the latter by which it may be understood in a universal and allegorical sense.

4

The Digressions: Past through Allusion, Future through Prophecy

If the thematic significance of the battles with monsters in the main narrative may be seen as that continual moral opposition required in the world against the persistent evil of fratricide, infidelity, and all antisocial crimes, then Beowulf is at once the anachronistic embodiment of Christian social values and a greatly endowed, if mortal, Germanic warrior in pursuit of the inevitably mundane, although praiseworthy, goals of pagan thane and lord. In his exceptional moral tenacity in upholding the values of kinship, comitatus, and peace throughout the poem he suggests the ideal Christian knight and king. He opposes the forces of social destruction embodied in the monsters, who are, of course, while embodiments of evil, individual enemies physically threatening their frightened victims and must be fought and destroyed in defence not only of moral principle but of life and limb, as well. Beowulf himself enters the contest with this pragmatic purpose, and as has been said, it is only gradually that he perceives the common origin of these harassments and their moral-historical significance.

This wider significance embedded in the main narrative is illuminated through the poet's use of the Cain legend. In making the monsters the progeny of the first fratricide, he is not adapting a self-conscious literary myth but employing an ethical and temporal scheme universally subscribed to in the middle ages, lending to his poem the metaphysical dimensions of the moral history of mankind. Thus in Grendel and the dragon the medieval audience of the poem would be able to recognize the survival of Cain's monstrous progeny and the symbol of his sin in those who formed the bestial clan dedicated to the destruction of social harmony and brotherhood and determined to eradicate the Abels of the earth. Herein one discovered the unbroken historical line in which evil had been passed down from the initial unnatural act of the first spiller of blood to the very present time, still haunted and persecuted by the monstrous offspring of Cain. The monsters thus represent the actual perpetuation of Cain's evil in the form of physical menace. Because of the traditions that surround them with an air of the marvellous, the same monsters evoke the fabulous. Somewhat irrationally, as with much legend, the monsters are both of angelic origin and human, their sire both Cain and Satan. Grendel and the dragon are both actual and fabulous, generalized rather than fictionalized, as representative of historical and moral fact.

The same theme of the evil spirit of Cain and the opposition to it is carried out on another level of the poem, for in the so-called digressions we see an extension of the idea to the modes of past and future history. These historical episodes, which constitute a considerable portion of the poem, extend the scriptural idea of moral history beyond the epoch of biblical time to the immediate past of the German nations and find in that history a corroboration of the scriptural and exegetical idea of the continuity of evil. They also provide a contemporary historic complement to the moral significance of Grendel and the dragon. In this manner the main action becomes a paradigm of the actions in the historical episodes and provides a universal explanation for them, relating Germanic history to that of Rome, Greece, Israel, and Eden.

The historical episodes are, then, not really digressions from the main theme but rather the means by which that theme achieves full moral and social significance and aesthetic completion. Having as the setting of his poem the historic present of the Danish and Geatish courts, the poet has carefully structured the episodes to reveal the universal significance of events in the respective national pasts and futures, moving out from the main theme periodically to past allusions and future prophecies in which signs already present in the main theme may find their mirror reflection in these episodes. The general facts of the Geatish and Danish past would have been known to an Anglo-Saxon audience since they constituted a history of interest to that audience. Thus the future as the poet reports it in *Beowulf* is recognizable to the audience as part of its own more recent past, and, setting itself in the present of the poem, the audience is able to accept as prophecy the allusions to the future, knowing, of course, that they have already been fulfilled. Having managed his poem and his audience in this way, the poet is able to reveal the ethical significance of history with the authority of history itself. Thus the episodes cover three Scandinavian sagas prior to Hrothgar's reign: the stories of Heremod, Sigemund, and Finnsburg. As R.W. Chambers has claimed, it is clear that in the literature and minds of Teutonic people a strong connection existed between Heremod and Sigemund,[1] and it is through this connection that the Sigemund episode seemed to form a part of the Danish past. Along with these are the prophecies concerning the Danish future: the treachery of Hrothulf and Unferth and the story of Freawaru.

Similar structuring may be noted in the handling of the tragedy of the Geatish nation. The past events of Haethcyn's fratricide, the Swedish wars, and the story of Eormanric extend the main theme to the past of this nation. Its future is evoked in the closing prophecy of the destruction of the Geats under Wiglaf. Thus the theme of the spirit of Cain described in these episodes, including historical examples from several Germanic nations at different moments in time, is presented not as a particular malady of an evil nation but as a fundamental part of the universal human social condition. Spanning past, present, and future of the time of the poem, the theme of the episodes seems to transcend time as well as place, and unlimited as it is to a particular nation, the evil of social discord is seen as part of the eternal human struggle.

On the level of the poem represented by the episodes, the children of Cain are not physical monsters but human beings who perpetuate Cain's sin, becoming his sons by adopting his spiritual disposition. Thus the transition between history and allegory is accomplished in such a way that characters are simultaneously engaged on both levels.

Heremod is one of Cain's tropological children brought into the poem initially as a foil to Beowulf, as is Sigemund. The comparison begins first with the story of Sigemund, which as presented in *Beowulf* seems to have a rather clear theme – the virtue of kinship. The blood relationship between Sigemund and Fitela ('eam his nefan,' 881) is a central feature of the tale. Uncle and nephew are called 'companions in need' ('nydgestellan,' 882) and are joined in opposition to the 'eotena cyn,' for as the poet tells us, they had slain many of the race of monsters with swords:

'Hæfdon ealfela   eotena cynnes
sweordum gesæged.' (883–4)

There is perhaps some suggestion that their kinship and struggle come to fulfilment in their opposition to the 'eotena cyn.' Among the race of monsters so designated would seem to be included the rather special 'wrætlicne wyrm' (891) whose defeat brought Sigemund everlasting fame. One might point out the factors that seem especially emphasized in the poet's rendition of the tale: the kin fidelity of uncle and nephew, their war against the 'eotena cyn,' and Sigemund's slaying of the dragon. If the Sigemund story is meant as a foil to Beowulf, one may wonder at the propriety of the comparison. Beowulf has just slain a troll, not a dragon; he has neither sister nor sister-son. In what way, then, do these factors of the Sigemund story contribute to Beowulf's fame?

One cannot say with certainty how much of the traditional story of Sigemund was known to the *Beowulf* poet and his audience, but one might suggest the points in the older tradition that seem to have relevance to the episode in the poem. In the *Volsungasaga* Sigemund appears as the chief actor in a story of parricide and vengeance. His sister is married to a foreign king, Siggeirr of Gautland, and during a visit paid to Gautland by Signy's father, King Volsungr, Siggeirr attacks and kills his father-in-law and brothers-in-law. Sigemund alone escapes and later, with the help of his sister, vanquishes the treacherous Siggeirr. It is perhaps possible that this background of parricide is one of the elements that attracted the *Beowulf* poet to the tale of Sigemund and caused him to include it in connection with the Heremod story in the poem.

If such is the case, the comparison with Beowulf is fitting. Through the depiction of his relation to Hygelac, his youthful history, and especially his fight with Grendel, Beowulf has already been established as revering kinship and opposing the crime of Cain. In Grendel's lineage and the general Cain tradition, it is seen that 'eotens,' as giants, are among the children of Cain and that Grendel himself is one of them. Thus Sigemund's battle against the 'eotena cynne' (883) provides an excellent parallel for Beowulf's defeat of the 'eoten' in Denmark descended from the father of parricide and war. Sigemund not only slays a monstrous 'marpeace' in the form of the dragon, but, if tradition is invoked in the allusion, he is also the opponent of the human moral offspring of Cain, one of whom has killed his father and brothers.

Beowulf is further praised by his dissimilarity to Heremod, and indirectly, as well, by Sigemund's dissimilarity to Heremod, since there are actually two comparisons being drawn. From the negative portrait of Heremod we are provided with a description of what the good lord and ethical man ought not to be, and by deducing the opposite of this portrait the audience may perceive the values the poet wishes to advance. The salient theme of the episode is once again a social one, concerning the comitatus relationship that grew out of the kinship institution and was analogous to it. Thus as Sigemund and his nephew were the ideal representatives of kin and comitatus fidelity, Heremod is an example of evil violation of the bond.

Heremod's story, like Cain's, is one of a man greatly favoured by God but at last overcome by the spirit of enmity and bloodthirstiness.[2] The poet tells us that he oppressed his people; 'aldorceare' (906), or life sorrow, suggests murderous oppression, a suggestion later confirmed by Hrothgar's words:

'Ne geweox he him to willan,   ac to wælfealle
ond to deaðcwalum   Deniga leodum;
breat bolgenmod   beodgeneatas,
eaxlgesteallan,   oþ þæt he ana hwearf,
mære þeoden   mondreamum from.' (1711–15)

Heremod's crime, the slaughter of table companions and faithful retainers, is equivalent to parricide in the way that regicide is equivalent to parricide. The effect of his crime is to place the Danes in the perilous state of lordlessness feared by all nations:

Se þe him bealwa to   bote gelyfde,
þæt þæt ðeodnes bearn   geþeon scolde,
fæderæþelum onfon,   folc gehealdan. (909–11)

Furthermore, Chambers has pointed out the evidence for the identification of Heremod and Lotherus, and to the extent that this connection is valid, some kind of kin violation seems to be involved, as well. In *Saxo Grammaticus* 1: 10–11, the Heremod-Lotherus story is suggestive of the Adam-Eve, Cain-Abel legend of Genesis.[3] Dan, progenitor of the Danish kings, sired two sons by Grytha: Humble and Lother. Humble became king upon the death of his father, but the throne was taken from him by force by his own brother. Lother proved a stingy and bloodthirsty king and was soon removed by his people. Lother is in the Germanic legend the younger brother, although his character suggests the elder brother in the Judaeo-Christian story. The characteristics attributed to Lother here suggest a confusion of identity in other stories about Heremod. In *Beowulf* the description of Heremod is remarkably like that of Lother in *Saxo Grammaticus*. The fact that Heremothr in the *Gylfaginning* is described as Baldr's brother and Lotherus (Heremothr) in Messenius is assigned the responsibility for killing this brother to obtain the crown provides another suggestion about the fundamentally fratricidal nature of Heremod's evil.

The other features of the episode as recounted in *Beowulf* tend to confirm these suggestions. For crimes against his retainers Heremod suffers the punishment that exegetical tradition describes Cain as under-going and which Anglo-Saxon law consistently prescribed for fratricides: he is exiled. Heremod, like Cain and Grendel, dwelt 'mandreamum from' (1715), preserving an echo of the poet's description of Cain, 'mandream fleon' (1264). Also similar to the description of Cain in exegesis, Heremod is stingy and greedy: 'Nallas beagas geaf / Denum æfter dome' (1719–20). In both cases these vices of greed and stinginess lead to violations of social bonds.

Just as Grendel endures a cheerless abode cut off from the joy of society because he is a descendant of Cain, so, too, Heremod's exile is described: 'Dreamleas gebad, / þæt he þæs gewinnes weorc þrowade' (1720–1). More precisely, he is exiled amid those mysterious people who among other things are described earlier as part of Cain's monstrous descent: 'He mid Eotenum wearð / on feonda geweald forð forlacen' (902–3). Heremod, it would seem, like many sinners described in exegesis, followed in the way of Cain and his kin, worshipped the giants by adopting their spirit of enmity, and commemorated the fratricidal evil of Cain's clan. It is probably in this sense and by his own sinfulness that 'he became like the "eotens," misled into the power of fiends.'

Recently the reading of 'eoten' as Jute has been widely challenged and, considering that the interpretation rests on the assumption of scribal error and a seventeenth-century reference to Lotherus in Messenius, it is natural to wish to find a more solid one. A fuller discussion of the reading of 'eoten' is be found in the discussion of the Finnsburg episode. But in relation to the Heremod story one is bound to remark that even if there were historical and textual evidence to support the Jute reading (which there is not), it would be a strange and sudden irrelevance on the part of the poet to introduce the tribe into the story. In the normal meaning of the term as the giants descended from Cain, the 'eotens' are thematically relevant in the Heremod tale and consistent in the context. Heremod, as a parricidal ruler, suffers the fate of Cain, the first parricide, and is exiled. He has gone the way of the 'eotens,' or is exiled among the 'eotens,' who like Grendel are perpetual exiles. One may accept in general the reading of N.F. Blake: 'He was seduced [from God and consequently] quickly dispatched into the power of devils, among the giants. He was racked by painful sufferings of fire for ever.'[4]

The third allusion to the Danish historical past is found in the Finnsburg episode, and again we are presented with a saga of parricide, vengeance, and social strife. Still within the context of Beowulf's victory over Grendel, the scop of Heorot, likely the same who has told the tales of Sigemund and of Heremod, introduces a story of a similar theme: 'Ne huru Hildeburh, herian þorfte / Eotena treowe' (1071–2). He goes on to tell the nature of the misery for which these 'eotens' are responsible. As the wife of Finn, Hildeburh is the nexus that joins two clans in mutual kinship and makes Hnaef and Finn brothers. The cause of the enmity that the tale depicts is not given, but it was probably well known to the poet's audience. This much, however, is clear: it was in some way attributable to the 'eotens.' Finn's attack upon his in-laws is one more example of the parricidal crime that blemishes the history of the Germanic nations. The result in this case is the destruction of a royal house and the tragic anguish of a queen.[5] The nature of Hildeburh's suffering is vividly and economically brought out in the beginning of the tale:

Unsynnum wearð
beloren leofum   æt þam lindplegan
bearnum ond broðrum;   hie on gebyrd hruron
gare wunde;   þæt wæs geomuru ides! (1072–5)

In these few lines the tragedy of pagan society is crystallized and the insoluble moral dilemma of parricide is fully expressed. Hildeburh's son and her brother fought on opposite sides, and one may even have been the killer of the other. The grieving mother can find no solace in thoughts of avenging her son, nor the grieving sister in hopes of recompense, the two consolations offered by pagan society. The spirit of enmity, probably originating in an ancient feud between the two clans, has triumphed over the bonds of kinship as it so often did in pagan ethics, and the moral suffering it causes is startlingly perceived in the image of Hildeburh as bereaved mother, sister, and ultimately wife. Its social costs are expressed in the spectacle of the destruction of the Frisian community.

It is in this sense that the 'eotens' play a role in the tragedy at Finnsburg. Earlier in the poem they have been clearly described as the offspring of Cain, the monster progeny that perpetuate the evil introduced into the world by the first murderer. Also, just as Grendel and his dam, who were 'eotens,' persecuted the peaceful society of the Danes, Heremod before him persecuted that society, as well, and for his evil deeds ended up with the 'eotens' in the pains of hell. So now in Finnsburg the spirit of enmity and fratricide that destroys society is traced to the 'eotens.' Whether the poet intends to indicate that the Cain-like, or 'eotenisc,' spirit was to be blamed on the Danish or Frisian side is left ambiguous in the poem and lost to us in history, but the violent emendation of the sense of the word 'eoten' to mean Jute instead of giant or monster is not here or elsewhere consistent with the rest of the poem or the sense of the passage.

Kaske's study of the 'eoten' examines the figurative use of the word and produces what one would consider far better results for the literary critic: 'A resulting possibility is that *eotena* and *eotenum* may be used in the Finn episode as an insulting figurative epithet for enemies.'[6] This sense he sees as borne out by evidence from exegesis identifying the giants as enemies of God and mankind.

While Kaske's approach to the problem is refreshingly imaginative and makes much better poetic sense of the episode, he may not go far enough in pursuing the identity of the 'eotens' in exegetical legend, and the resulting sense of 'enemies' as the identification may be too general. In *Beowulf* the poet has several occasions to describe enemies, yet the word 'eoten' seems reserved for a special kind. Especially if we consider the use of the word in all its appearances throughout the poem, the figurative epithet of 'enemy,' arising as it does out of an exegetical text, may require more precision and detail.

If one attempts to work with the word as we find it in the text without emendation and accepts its normal West-Saxon meaning, a more poetically integrated sense may be forthcoming. The word occurs nine times in various uncompounded forms and four times in compounds throughout *Beowulf*. Only five of these thirteen occurrences have historically caused confusion and demanded special explanation – the four occurrences in the Finn episode and the single occurrence in the Heremod story. The use of the word in the Heremod episode has been discussed. The remaining four uses of it in the Finn story are important enough to call for some examination.

Within the context of the exegetical tradition of Cain that we have been describing and the thematic and structural character that has been suggested for *Beowulf*, the Finnsburg episode reveals a harmonious relationship with the rest of the poem if we permit the regular and complete meaning of 'eoten' as Cain-descended giants. By a perception of the historic and symbolic functions of these creatures the Finn story emerges as relevant both to the main theme of the poem and to the other historical episodes.

Readers of *Beowulf* have long been impressed by the dramatic force of the opening image of Hildeburh lamenting her fate and pondering her own tragic ambivalence. Like the old warrior whose son is hanged, she is inconsolable. If, as we are sometimes told, the blame for the war has been clearly placed on one party or the other and Hildeburh is aware of which party is guilty, the tragic nature of the situation is diminished. It would seem more likely that what the queen laments as she views the carnage of her kin is the fundamental moral weakness that leads men to hostility and fratricide, the failure of love of which she is a symbol. As the peace and kinship of Hrothgar's house is plagued by an 'eoten,' so is that of Hildeburh, and it is thus the same bloodthirsty race and its spirit of fratricide that she condemns at the outset of the episode.

After the fratricidal encounter between Finn and the Danes, the 'morþbealo maga' (1079) that Hildeburh sees at dawn, both sides are reduced to a point where further combat is impossible, and a treaty is struck. The difficulty we have in trying to understand how such a treaty could be made is due to the ethical prohibition against making peace with the slayer of one's lord. This difficulty is somewhat diminished by evidence from history and law where we discover that such a solution could actually be accepted in the pragmatism of human affairs. However, we also know that vengeance was a persistent force and that the results seen at the end of the story were usual enough.

A treaty is made between Finn and the Danes because no other alternative exists. So the poet specifies the conditions set forth:

> Ac hig him geþingo budon,
> þæt hie him oðer flet   eal gerymdon,
> healle ond heahsetl,   þæt hie healfre geweald
> wið Eotena bearn   agan moston,
> ond æt feohgyftum   Folcwaldan sunu
> dogra gehwylce   Dene weorþode,
> Hengestes heap   hringum wenede
> efne swa swiðe   sincgestreonum
> fættan goldes,   swa he Fresena cyn
> on beorsele   byldan wolde.
> Ða hie getruwedon   on twa healfa
> fæste frioðuwære. (1085–96)

The 'eotens,' who at the outset of the story are charged with inspiring the enmity between Danes and Frisians, are again mentioned in the terms of the treaty. Finn offers (1) to provide another hall; (2) to provide, with the Danes, protection of the hall against the 'eotens' ('healfre geweald / wið Eotena bearn');[7] and (3) to distribute rewards equally among the Danes and the Frisians.[8]

The first clause of Finn's proposal, an 'oðer flet,' can refer to a hall separate from Finn's. But 'oðer' ought more normally to mean a second or new hall; since we know that Finn's hall has been destroyed by fire in the battle, it seems more likely that 'oðer flet' is meant to indicate a replacement for it, 'another hall,' and in that case the Danes and Frisians are meant to share the new hall together.

The second of Finn's clauses is less easily understood. If we assume that the 'eotena bearn' as a third party of Jutes is responsible for the treachery that had led to war, it is quite inconceivable that Finn, who is anxious for peace, would suggest housing these treacherous enemies with the vengeance-prone Danes. W.W. Lawrence, arguing from the weaker position of Finn ('Wig ealle fornam / Finnes ðegnas,' 1080–1), feels a certain dissatisfaction that none of the terms of the treaty makes requirements upon the Danes, but each is a concession to them.[9] This, of course, is true only if one regards 'eotena bearn' as Jutes or as the Frisians themselves. The problem is reduced if we restore the normal meaning of the word. In so doing we see that the words 'þæt hie healfre geweald / wið Eotena bearn agan moston' constitute a mutual promise to keep the peace and thus make demands on both sides. Having established the role of the 'eotens' in the first line of the episode as the origin of enmity, the poet now goes on logically to describe the peace treaty as one that requires both the Danes and the Frisians as hall companions to protect and guard this new brotherhood against the spirit of enmity that originally caused hostility. Understanding the basic meaning of 'wið' as opposition, the line would then read: 'That they [the Danes] might provide the protection of half the hall against the giant progeny.'[10] The other 'half' of the resistance is up to the Frisians. That the responsibility for peace is shared by two parties – the Frisians and the Danes – is again emphasized in the conclusion of the pact: 'Ða hie getruwedon on twa healfa / fæste frioðuwære.'

Finn's third clause provides for the Danes' receiving as much in the way of gifts and spoils as the Frisians. What, then, about the Jutes? If there is a third party important enough to be allowed to share half power with the Danes, they surely are not going to put up with being shut out of the spoils! Simple consistency would require the poet to state that the Danes and the Jutes will receive as much as the Frisians. Nor does the identification of 'eotena bearn' with the Frisians help matters, for it is unlikely as a point of style, although not impossible, that the poet would in one clause of the treaty refer to them as 'eotena bearn' and in another as 'Fresena cyn.' One must observe that this is not an example of Anglo-Saxon litotes, for the names occur in entirely different contexts and the poet seems to be indicating two different ideas. The enmity and the attempt at peace involve neither Jutes nor any other third tribe, but only those children of Cain on both sides who, like the giants of Genesis, had become the moral progeny of their ancestor through perpetuation of his evil.

This role of the 'eotens' is continued in the description of the second outbreak of hostilities, which traces the growth of the desire for vengeance in the human heart:

> He to gyrnwræce
> swiðor þohte   þonne to sælade,
> gif he torngemot   þurhteon mihte,
> þæt he Eotena bearn   [inne] gemunde.
> Swa he ne forwyrnde [worold rædenne]. (1138–42)[11]

Lust for vengeance is expressed in the phrase 'Eotena bearn   [inne] gemunde'; and through Hengest's desire to 'remember within,' or commemorate, the 'eotena bearn,' the poet is describing the breaking of the treaty by the Danish warrior who had sworn to maintain resistance against this giant progeny. The bargain is broken in the same terms as those in which it was struck, and the Danes have failed in their half of the vigilance against war. The triumph of blood-lust in Hengest's mind – and, it would seem to be implied, in pagan society as a whole – is sadly signified by the statement 'Swa he ne forwyrnde   [worold rædenne]' (1142): 'Thus did he not resist the way of the world.'

Particularized in the Finn episode as in other historical allusions, 'the way of the world' is a salient aspect of the theme of the poem, just as the same idea in Augustine's *City of God*, the worldly ethics of power and bloodshed, is expressed through the figure of Cain. By following 'the way of the world' men and nations have fallen and been destroyed, as all of human history demonstrates. Hengest decides to dishonour the treaty he has sworn, to attack his kinsmen and widow his sister, because he is ever reminded of his duty to avenge Hnæf, the 'worold rædenne' of pagan society. Thus the passage might read: 'He to vengeance thought more eagerly than to sailing home, whether he might create hostility to commemorate the giant progeny; thus did he succumb to the way of the world.'

The spectacle of moral and social catastrophe continues directly with Hengest's acceptance of a sword 'þæs wæron mid Eotenum   ecge cuðe' (1145), which gesture goes far in creating an emblem expressive of Hengest's compromise with the world. As we know, 'ecge' was a word denoting the entire sword and not the cutting edge only – a synonym for it.

That the sword as a weapon would be well known to the giants is not surprising, for its use is in complete harmony with the exegetical tradition that the *Beowulf* poet has relied on elsewhere in the poem for symbolic vocabulary. That tradition assigned the discovery of swords to Tubal-Cain and the giants for the further undermining of civilization. It is highly suitable and lightly ironic that the instrument by which the evil of Cain will be perpetuated in Finnsburg is introduced as well known among a brood seen in legend as descending from him. The 'eotena bearn,' then, would seem to be all those men not further identified who urge others on both sides to break peace, shed blood, and assault thus the foundation of civilization. The phrase may be taken as designating both individuals morally akin to Cain and a general moral disposition, a social spirit, the results of which are seen in the Finnsburg tragedy.

It is, of course, possible in this passage that the poet is going further in identifying the guilty party in the renewal of hostilities by homonymically employing 'eoten' to create a pun on 'Jute' – 'giant'; or even, as Kaske has suggested, introducing the term as an insulting designation of Hengest's enemies, the Frisians. Such a view does not contradict the general sense used here of 'eoten' as Cain-descended giant, but it is not my interpretation. I can see no convincing evidence that 'eoten' in *Beowulf* ever means Jutes, but rather persuasive evidence of internal consistency that it always means giants.

Thus, like the Sigemund story and the Heremod episodes, the Finn story is one of the three sagas of Danish and Scandinavian past that extend the theme of social harmony, kinship, and comitatus to the historical level. Like the Heremod episode, it is a tale of the violation of these values and the triumph of the evil of Cain in fratricide and vengeance. The function and value of 'friðusibb,' the peace bond, was that through marriage it made brothers of enemies by incorporating them into the same clan. This at least was the hope of civilized men, but as we see in the story of Finn, the persistence of opposite values frequently triumphed over those of honour, family, and love.

The episodes of the Geatish past are, like those of the Danish, three in number. The first of these allusions is to the Hæthcyn story in which it is indicated that the foundations of the house of Hrethel are stained with brother's blood and that the theme of fratricide is present, as well, in Geatish history:

'Wæs þam yldestan   ungedefelice
mæges dædum   morþorbed stred,

syþþan hyne Hæðcyn   of hornbogan,
his freawine   flane geswencte,
miste mercelses   ond his mæg ofscet,
broðor oðerne,   blodigan gare.
Ðæt wæs feohleas gefeoht,   fyrenum gesyngad,
hreðre hygemeðe;   sceolde hwæðre swa þeah
æðeling unwrecen   ealdres linnan.' (2435–43)

The question of Hæthcyn's guilt is left undecided in the text. We have
Beowulf's description of the crime as shameful ('ungedefelice'), and the
actor as sinning criminally ('fyrenum gesyngad'). On the other hand we are
told that Hæthcyn 'miste mercelses,' and thus it is a problem of balancing
one statement against the other. The statements in lines 2435 and 2441 as
well as the use of the word 'morðorbed' might persuade us to regard line
2439 as irony typical of the *Beowulf* poet, for we are not assured that
Hæthcyn intended, when he missed the mark, to hit it in the first place.

It is not, however, the accidental or intentional quality of the act that is
primary in the incident, but its fratricidal character. Medieval ecclesiastical
law punished accidental fratricide as a crime, and the sentence was usually
equal to that for intentional homicide.[12] This may be due to the fact that the
results of the crime to society, regardless of intention, were the same.
Further, Hæthcyn's crime is not restricted to fratricide. The poet does not
let us forget that Herebeald was not only Hæthcyn's brother but also his
future lord and king of the Geats; thus the crime was a double one involving
fratricide and regicide.[13]

The parable told by Beowulf of the sorrowful old knight whose son is
hanged illustrates at once the general and the particular grief of fratricide
and vengeance. The frequent breakdown of the moral obligation of kinship,
which was employed as a bulwark of peace in a half-converted society, is
shown in Hæthcyn's crime and Hrethel's anguish. When the sole solution
and consolation of murder is vengeance, as it was in pagan society, the
fratricide could escape all punishment and, like Hæthcyn, even succeed to
his victim's heritage. Thus Hrethel must accept the failure of pagan justice
and contemplate his heir's murderer as he assumes his brother's inheritance. Hrethel's only consolation for the loss of a son would lie in vengeance
and the loss of another son. This being impossible, he gives up his life and
quits a world whose ethical structures cannot answer his moral needs.

So, too, the old knight of Beowulf's parable, steeped in the ethic of
vengeance, finds himself and his heathen society morally bankrupt in face
of another moral reality that includes the concept of justice. The knight's

son would seem to have been executed for a crime by the state and pays his debt to society. Because both the idea of a debt to society and the idea of forgoing vengeance conflict with the values of private justice, the old knight finds the situation intolerable.

The effect of Hæthcyn's crime on the Geatish nation is suggested as the origin of hostilities with Sweden. The concrete reason for Ongentheow's attack is not given, but it is said that the death of Hrethel was its occasion ('syððan Hreðel swealt,' 2474), and it is conceivable that the Swedes found an excuse in Hæthcyn's crime to refuse his claim to the throne and consider it open to seizure. At any rate, we have in the story of Hæthcyn the first episode in the history of the Geats, and it turns out to be fratricidal.

The saga of the Swedish wars is another episode in national history in which the Swedes are the aggressors. An invasion of Sweden by the Geats follows the initial aggression during which Hæthcyn is killed and Hygelac becomes king:

> Þæt mægwine   mine gewræcan,
> fæhðe and fyrene,   swa hyt gefræge wæs,
> þeah ðe oðer his   ealdre gebohte,
> heardan ceape;   Hæðcynne wearð,
> Geata dryhtne   guð onsæge.' (2479–83)

Hæthcyn's death is paid for when Ongentheow is killed in the skirmish with two brothers, Wulf and Eofor. To this point we are perhaps dealing with simple battle, but events occurring after the death of Ongentheow bring the episode of the Swedish wars into thematic relation with other historical narratives, for this is the beginning of Onela's parricidal dispute with his nephews, Eanmund and Eadgils, Ongentheow's sons – a dispute that will entail the deaths of Eanmund, Onela, and Heardred and will ultimately be the seed of the destruction of the Geats. The details of the Swedish internecine feud have been discussed earlier in connection with Heardred's downfall and Beowulf's accession to throne, and the parricidal nature of the conflict was noted.

In relation to Hygelac's death we have also discussed the past-historical context of the Brosing necklace, a potential symbol of kin murder. Eormanric was apparently the murderer of his nephews and his own son. Eormanric became, as Klaeber tells us, a symbol in poetry of 'a ferocious, covetous, and treacherous tyrant.'[14] He is thus a kind of counterpart of Heremod related to the Geatish past. The necklace as the object of his covetousness recalls perhaps the myth of jewels and precious metals as associated with irrational passion and the fall of civilization.

The two allusions to the Danish future similarly involve the failure of that society to secure peace, despite the defeat of the physical monsters that plagued it, and the ultimate triumph of the spirit of Cain. Beowulf presents a muted picture of his own triumph to Hygelac upon his return home in prophesying the failure of Freawaru as peace bond. As A.G. Brodeur has pointed out, the Beowulf poet deliberately obscures and generalizes the account of Ingeld's vengeance in order to impart to it the imprecision of prediction. As he relates the Freawaru-Ingeld episode, the poet assigns the renewing of the quarrel to a nameless young warrior. The audience, however, since it knows the details and the outcome, could identify Ingeld as the real perpetrator of the crime: 'It follows that our poet chose to obscure the acting personages of the story as he and his audience knew it, and that he did so for a specific artistic purpose. In so doing, he could count on recognition by his hearers of the nature and the purpose of his procedure.'[15]

Part of that purpose is certainly the striking contrast between youth and age. We know from historical sources that the Danish-Heathobard feud was an ancient one originating two generations before Ingeld and Freawaru. The episode in *Beowulf* is one of violation of peace and kinship inspired by an old warrior whose very ancientness is suggestive of the old and hidden crimes of the past:

'Ðonne cwið æt beore   se ðe beah gesyhð,
eald æscwiga,   se ðe eall gem(an),
garcwealm gumena   – him bið grim sefa – ,
onginneð geomormod   geong(um) cempan
þurh hreðra gehygd   higes cunnian,
wigbealu weccean.' (2041–6)

Thus the grim-minded man, a man of the old way who remembers all, poisons the mind of the young warrior, blissfully unaware of feud, as they sit in the midst of a friendly and peaceful band. The ancient ethic of blood and vengeance personified by the old warrior is passed on through constant goading to the innocent youth, and peace and kinship are destroyed.

The parricidal nature of the Freawaru episode is suggested in *Beowulf* and borne out in history. Healfdene had been killed by Froda, his death was avenged by Hrothgar and his brothers, and Froda perished through this vengeance. It is interesting that Scandinavian sources make this feud, which is the origin of the later catastrophe, a fratricidal one between two brothers of the Scylding family.[16] Upon attaining the throne of Denmark, however, Hrothgar in characteristic peacefulness seeks to end the feud by uniting the two tribes through the marriage of his daughter, Freawaru, to Ingeld. Thus the Heathobards and Danes are kinsmen through marriage, and it is about the efficacy of this kinship in the face of the spirit of revenge that Beowulf makes his prediction.

The waste and injustice of the crime is economically expressed in the description of the Danish youth's death: 'þæt se fæmnan þegn   fore fæder dædum / æfter billes bite   blodfag swefeð' (2059–60). In that act of vengeance the spirit of the old ethic destroys all oaths of peace and kinship:

'Þonne bioð (ab)rocene   on ba healfe
aðsweord eorla;   (syð)ðan Ingelde
weallað wælniðas,   ond him wiflufan
æfter cearwælmum   colran weorðað.
Þy ic Heaðo-Bear[d]na   hyldo ne telge,
dryhtsibbe dæl   Denum unfæcne.' (2063–8)

The failure of Freawaru as peace bond had still further significance in Danish history of which Beowulf at the moment of his prophecy was unaware. As is known from historical sources, the feud between the Danes and Heathobards, once rekindled, resulted in the destruction of Heorot to which the poet has already alluded earlier in the poem:

Heaðowylma bad,
laðan liges; ne wæs hit lenge þa gen,
þæt se ecghete   aþumsweoran,
æfter wælniðe   wæcnan scolde. (82–5)

Thus the symbol of social harmony, kinship, and peace is destroyed through the parricidal war of Ingeld against Hrothgar. The reality behind that symbol is soon afterwards destroyed through the parricidal treachery of Hrothulf in apparent conspiracy with the treacherous fratricide Unferth. This allusion to the Hrothulf-Unferth plot constitutes the second allusion to the Danish future.

While historical analogues may have limited corroborative value, all evidence tends to the view that Hrothulf did not wait until Hrothgar's death to seize the Danish throne from Hrethric, but murdered both his uncle and cousin together. A.A. Lee takes the view that Unferth and Hrothulf are unquestionably implicated in a treasonous act,[17] and Kemp Malone points out that all Scandinavian evidence indicates Hrothgar was murdered by a kinsman. Moreover, Hrothulf's murder of his cousin Hrethric seems to be historically verifiable.[18] Thus it would appear that we have once again the evocation of a historical episode with a theme of parricide leading to national catastrophe.

The involvement of Unferth in this future treachery is discerned through subtle intimations by the *Beowulf* poet, strong enough, however, to be remarkable; this is quite in addition to his role as evil counsellor, which is paralleled elsewhere. The first and chief of these ironies is created through his very introduction into a scene pregnant with allusions to future betrayal. The use of the ominous 'gyt' (1164) serves to juxtapose the ironic allusions to treachery and the very name of Unferth (1165). There is something especially sinister in the scene in which the fratricide Unferth sits at the feet of the future parricide Hrothulf and his victim, Hrothgar:

Sæton suhtergefæderan;   þa gyt wæs hiera sib ætgædere,
æghwylc oðrum trywe.   Swylce þær Unferþ þyle
æt fotum sæt frean Scyldinga;   gehwylc hiora his ferhþe treowde,
þæt he hæfde mod micel,   þeah þe he his magum nære
arfæst æt ecga gelacum. (1164–8)

Unferth's character suggests nothing contrary to such treacherous potential. When introduced he was attempting to prevent Beowulf from cleansing Heorot of Grendel. He then tried to discredit the Geat's credentials for such a mission. Beowulf's stinging retort on that occasion, which included the charge of fratricide, silenced his foe:

'Þeah ðu þinum broðrum   to banan wurde,
heafodmægum;   þæs þu in helle scealt
werhðo dreogan,   þeah þin wit duge.' (587–9)

Unferth, then, can be taken as a kind of Cain; and to the audience of *Beowulf*, having been reminded of the exegetical legend of Cain only four hundred lines earlier, so he must have seemed. It is perhaps not surprising that his role in the poem includes an attempt to prevent the destruction of the Cain-descended monster who ravages the brotherhood of Heorot. As Brodeur has noted,[19] there is something quite other than loss of face that Unferth fears from Beowulf's attack on Grendel, for being 'thyle' at Heorot he is under no obligation to assume the role of warrior himself. Instead it would seem that Unferth through his crime against kin has gone the way of Cain, like Heremod, and his attempt to discredit Beowulf arises not so much out of jealousy as out of the desire to see Hrothgar's court weakened. What Unferth fears from Beowulf is that he will achieve peace, and this is not a state that Unferth enjoys nor that much favours his ambitions. As we see, although Grendel is defeated, the enmity between Hrothulf and Hrothgar brings in its wake parricide, regicide, and the fall of the Heorot – a goal that Grendel pursued.

In discussing the poet's description of Unferth as a fratricide in the court of Hrothgar (1017b–19), Brodeur concludes: 'The immediate adjunction of the statement about Unferth, *in this context*, can be nothing else than a clear intimation that he is to have a hand in fomenting the revolt [of Hrothulf against Hrothgar], and perhaps in its bloody consequences. This was pointed out long ago by Olrik; it has been stressed again and again, by Chambers, by Malone, and by Lawrence.'[20]

It seems to me entirely plausible and certainly in conformity with the text that Unferth and Hrothulf are already in league when Beowulf arrives in Denmark, and that Unferth sees in the devastation of Heorot by Grendel a means to a treasonous end. This would explain his anger at Beowulf's intention to destroy the monster and would call sharply into question his motives in lending the hero a sword that fails. In this sense Unferth is in league with the monsters, for what they fail to accomplish in their attacks he later accomplishes through treachery. Otherwise we must adopt the less-than-satisfactory view that Unferth is a character described as evil in the past as a fratricide, evil in the present as an opponent to Beowulf's match with Grendel, and evil in the future in his treason, but described in a single instance, when he lends his sword, as generous, magnanimous, and full of goodwill.

The loan of his sword to Beowulf for the fight with Grendel's dam must also be interpreted in relation to Unferth's total role. Despite Beowulf's own rather lavish praise of the weapon, it remains that this sword loaned by a fratricide for battle against a descendant of Cain not only fails Beowulf, but fails with almost mortal consequences. It is widely recognized that Beowulf is not an omniscient hero. His prophecy concerning Freawaru demonstrates a degree of awareness about the moral nature of his society, but in its very imprecision it also illustrates that this awareness is based on mortal common sense, not prophetic powers.

Hrothulf apparently holds a position in the Danish court similar to that of co-regent. Unlike his cousin Heoroweard, he possesses no precise legal claim to the throne since his father, Halga, the youngest of Healfdene's sons, had never been king. Why Heoroweard did not inherit his father's crown is not explained. The kindness and generosity of Hrothgar and Wealhtheow towards Hrothulf do not apparently arise from any fear of his superior claim to the throne, nor from guilty conscience, but from the simple spirit of kinship and goodwill that Hrothgar demonstrates consistently.

One of the fine contrasts of the poem is that of the relationship of Beowulf and his uncle Hygelac to the relationship of Hrothulf and his uncle Hrothgar. Of Beowulf's fidelity much is seen throughout the poem. Of the ominously silent Hrothulf we know from Wealhtheow's plea for her children that this character is feared by an anxious queen and mother. Unlike Hygd, she cannot count on good faith. It does not seem adequate to the poem's subtlety and irony to state, as Kenneth Sisam has, that Wealhtheow 'is sure that, if Hrothgar dies first, Hrothulf will ''take good care of the young men''.'[21] Wealhtheow's long reminder to Hrothulf of the kindness shown to him by Hrothgar is much more in the form of a plea than a declaration of assurance. From that address to Hrothulf (1180–7) she turns to Beowulf, dramatically seated between her two sons, and in strong terms enlists his protection for them as she bedecks him with treasure. The 'plain reading' of the poem urged by Sisam is in this case so plain as to threaten to strip the passage of its meaning and drama.

Thus the two great comitatus relationships of the poem contrast sharply in the moral conditions of their younger members, as they do, perhaps, in those of the elder members, as well. As has been said, Hrothulf's treachery is clearly prophesied in *Beowulf* and recorded in historical legend. It was not long after the war with Ingeld – when, one would think, Denmark would have been at her weakest point – that Hrothulf and Unferth dethroned old Hrothgar and slew him with his son. The first intimations of Hrothulf's parricidal intentions are ominously placed in the context of Beowulf's victory over Grendel – almost, it would seem, as a qualification of it. This exposure of the moral disease of the Danish court lies squarely between the telling of the episodes of Heremod and Finnsburg, as if to suggest an extension into the future Danish history of their themes of past kin violation, bad faith, and vengeance:

> 'Ne gefrægen ic þa mægþe   maran weorode
> ymb hyra sincgyfan   sel gebæran.
> Bugon þa to bence   blædagande,
> fylle gefægon;   fægere geþægon

medoful manig   magas þara
swiðhicgende   on sele þam hean,
Hroðgar and Hroþulf.   Heorot innan wæs
freondum afylled;   nalles facenstafas
Þeod-Scyldingas   þenden fremedon.' (1011–19)

The picture of uncle and nephew sharing mead and kinship, the hall filled with friends, is shatteringly qualified by the 'þenden' of the final line with an effect not unlike that of the 'gyt' (1164) that deflates the familial scene of the same court. We are now made aware that a time will come when kinsmen will turn against each other. This suggestion is more forcibly presented directly after the recitation of the tale of Finn, when Unferth is introduced into the image of potential treachery. The placing of these two references to the fall of Hrothgar and his house as preface and conclusion to the Finnsburg episode can hardly be regarded as haphazard. The perception of the theme of fratricide and vengeance in the one alerts us to the variation of that theme in the other. Moreover, one must attribute a conscious intention to the poet in making these references to future Danish treachery and past kinship violation in Finnsburg the context of the moving plea of Wealh-theow.

Wealhtheow, as she fulfils the duties of courtesy in Hrothgar's court, has just heard the tale of Danish history filled with treason and slaughter of kin, and she, like the audience of *Beowulf*, perceives its universal application. Her words to Hrothgar reflect the general irony of the context:

'Heorot is gefælsod
beahsele beorhta;   bruc þenden þu mote
manigra medo,   one þinum magum læf
folc ond rice.' (1176–9)

Better than the queen can see, the audience, knowing what history has proven, can perceive that Wealhtheow is doomed to suffer a grief like Hildeburg's and that like her predecessor she will lose husband and son to the implacable spirit of Cain. Such prescience on the part of the audience lends to her motherly plea the pathos of futility and the irony of doom:

'Ic minne can
glædne Hroþulf,   þæt he þa geogoðe wile
arum healdan,   gyf þu ær þonne he,
wine Scildinga,   worold oflætest;

wene ic þæt he mid gode   gyldan wille
uncran eaferan,   gif he þæt eal gemon,
hwæt wit to willan   ond to worðmyndum
umborwesendum ær   arna gefremedon.' (1180–7)

How much Wealhtheow believes her own words and Hrothulf's
gratitude is shown when she feels it necessary to enlist Beowulf's aid in
guaranteeing her sons' future:

'Bruc ðisses beages,   Beowulf leofa,
hyse, mid hæle,   ond þisses hrægles neot,
þeo[d]gestreona,   ond geþeoh tela,
cen þec mid cræfte,   ond þyssum cnyhtum wes
lara liðe.' (1216–20)

In Wealhtheow's plea we see one of the finest poetic accomplishments of
the poem in its symbolizing of the extent in time of the tragic force of Cain.
Previously the poet has presented the plight of Hildeburg, a figure of the
remote Danish past whose queenly role of peacemaker placed her in
conflict with the ancient heathen ethic of blood vengeance, dooming her to
bewail the murder of husband, son, and father each at the hand of the other.
In the portrait of Wealhtheow the poet presents the spectacle of a Danish
queen of present time pleading against a history of parricide and revenge as
old as Cain and his kin, the contemporary force of which is strong enough to
overcome her plea and render her, too, a failure in her mission of peace.
Still later the poet completes the 'tragedy of queens' by predicting that the
future holds for Freawaru in her role as peacemaker the same grief and
failure as all Danish history witnesses. This image of misery is tri-mirrored
in the poem through past, present, and future in the sorrowful lives of three
noble Danish women. The force of such an image is to emphasize in the
moral and historical sense the Christian idea of the age-old evil passed
down from the first murderer through the race of monsters to the pagans
who enshrined as social institutions such evil practices as vengeance and
blood feud and worshipped the monsters as idols.

The king of Sweden at the time of Beowulf's death is Eadgils, who owes
his very life and rule to the dead king of the Geats, and quite naturally, this
debt has guaranteed peace between the two nations. How is it, then, that
the poet can have Beowulf's heir declare: 'Ne ic te Sweoðeode   sibbe oððe
treowe / wihte ne wene' (2922–3)? The reasons for this enmity reach far
back into the history of the two nations, and the more recent killing of

Ongentheow is the potential for new strife; but further, the renewal of hostilities and the destruction of the Geats seem to have their origins, like the other national disasters in the poem, in lust for vengeance. The message of future disaster is reported in the poem as: 'Wiglaf siteð / ofer Biowulfe, byre Wihstanes' (2906–7). Thus it is that in the very ascendency of the son of Weohstan the fate of the Geats is determined.

Like the warrior who accompanies Freawaru into Ingeld's court, innocent of the crimes that stain the weapons he carries, Wiglaf is presumably guilty of no man's blood:

> Ða wæs forma sið
> geongan cempan,   þæt he guðe ræs
> mid his freodryhtne   fremman sceolde. (2625–7)

However, the heritage that he bears, the inheritance from his father, marks him as a victim for vengeance. Weohstan, as we are informed earlier, slew Eanmund while in the service of Onela. It is his son who rules the Geats upon Beowulf's death. Eadgils, having determinedly avenged his father, would hardly forgo the opportunity of avenging his brother by striking at the son of his slayer. Adrien Bonjour presents the circumstances of the Wiglaf episode clearly and concisely:

Now if we remember that the circumstances of the Swedish wars were known by those for whom *Beowulf* was composed so that the poet might easily leave a certain number of things as understood, we can draw an extremely important conclusion. If Wiglaf's father, as 'leod Scylfinga', had fought on the side of Onela, the usurper, against the nephews Eanmund and Eadgils, who had fled to the Geats ... the overthrow and death of Onela carried with it a complete reversal of Weohstan's position. Indeed, 'After Eadgils had been established on the throne, Weohstan, who had slain Eanmund ... was compelled to leave the country and settled in the land of the Geats ...' Yet ... was it likely that the slaying of Eanmund would be definitely forgotten? Even if Weohstan had died, would not the probable hostility of Eadgils be transferred to his son?[22]

The future holds for the Geats the ancient malice of vengeance that was born of the seeds of parricide and regicide. Just as the courts and royal houses of the other nations of the poem have ultimately been destroyed through this antisocial force, so, too, the future destruction of Geatland will be brought about by the same force, regardless of personal innocence.

In such a manner does the theme transcend time and place to become a universal statement. As we have seen, the theme of parricide and vengeance extending to many royal houses and nations of the Germanic past widens its historical relevance and assumes universal proportions. In the same manner, the poet's device of extending the episodes that depict the crime of Cain to include both the historical past and future renders his picture of social tragedy as one not limited temporally but ever present in every human society. Through a combination of the two modes we are presented with a universalized image of a social and personal evil traditionally expressed through the figure of Cain and his progeny, passed down from generation to generation, civilization to civilization, lasting until the end of time itself.

5

Conclusion

To the medieval mind, which regarded history as a form of revelation, a pattern in the events unfolding in time could always be discovered, and the key to this pattern was to be found in Scripture, the other great source of revelation. The historical events recorded in the Old and New Testaments revealed a meaningful pattern that was true not only for the periods of time specifically dealt with in the Bible but for all epochs to the end of time. Thus an Anglo-Saxon Christian of the eighth or ninth century who was searching for an explanation of the apparent contradictions of his own social experience had a natural and profitable tendency to seek a theoretical basis for that explanation in Scripture and exegesis, since the meaning of present-historical experience had already been established in the patterns of events of past history. One of those patterns is found in the Cain and Abel story and its exegesis, in which discord and hate, first introduced by Satan, are perpetuated to the end of human history by those perverted souls who in their materialism and consequent bloodthirstiness allegorically become children of Cain.

Christian historians from the earliest moments of their activity shared this view of the past in different degrees. Its fullest expression is found in Augustine's *City of God*, which, although more polemical than historical in many aspects, develops a philosophy of history marked by the peculiarly successful integration of evil into Christian historical order, and it is this aspect that most widely influenced the middle ages. While Augustine is not interested in describing the weaknesses and crimes of the Christians in such a work, he nevertheless creates a theory of history that foresees the continuation of malice throughout time and the survival of an evil tradition without the negation of the ethical and spiritual ideals of Christianity. The basic image of *The City of God* is that of the coexistence and parallel development of good and evil forces from the beginning to the end of time. The most famous of Augustine's direct imitators was Orosius, who intentionally extended Augustine's thesis to his own national history. Orosius's work is the carrying out of the Augustine mission to rewrite history in the new dialectic and ultimately to Christianize time.

Thus it is not accurate to take Augustine's view as one that saw no good in pagan history at all. Naturally the polemical purpose of the composition required an emphasis on the failures of that civilization and prohibited focusing on its merits. Nevertheless the heart of Augustine's thesis is that from the beginning human history has been filled with Cains and with Abels. If Cain has been predominant in certain periods, Abel has never been completely absent.

Marie Padgett Hamilton discussed the possible influences of Augustine's *City of God* on *Beowulf* more than three decades ago, and her thesis deserves some renewed attention. According to Hamilton, 'the unifying principle in Augustine's view of history – the conception of Divine Providence as ruling all peoples from the beginning and as bestowing all gifts and graces – supplied a key to understanding the past of Germanic tribes, as well as that of the Hebrews or the pagan nations that are discussed in *The City of God*.'[1] While her view that the Christian concepts of grace and election also had significant and specific influence on *Beowulf* tends to lead us back to the unprofitable view of the poem as theological allegory, her perception of the similarity of the visions of history of the Anglo-Saxon poem and the Augustinian philosophy of history that had so wide a sphere of influence appears fundamentally correct. Hamilton rightly identifies as central themes of the poem the historical struggle against the forces of evil and the embodiment in the pagan hero of essential values of Christian civilization. The hero's opposition to Grendel and, through Grendel, to the race of Cain and its ethic is again the primary vehicle for the expression of the poet's theme, and this struggle, as Hamilton points out, did not begin with Christ or the Christians, but, as the student of Augustine would have known, was inherent in time itself: 'Beowulf's membership in the society of the just, needless to say, is implied in the persistent metaphor of his opposition to the kindred of Cain. He who wrestles with the powers of darkness naturally suggests "the most exalted hero-life known to Christians". The warfare against destruction with which the poem is concerned neither began nor ended with the magnanimous purging of Hrothgar's realm.'[2]

However, Hamilton passes over the historical allegory of the poem,[3] for she cannot understand how Grendel could be a historical descendant of

Cain. Thus she demotes him and his ilk to the rank of metaphor and, one must observe, in so doing diminishes the light she sheds on the poem.

Through the device of interlocking structures of temporal mode and of historical and fabulous action in *Beowulf* emerges a panorama of the devastation of pagan societies unlimited in time and place, at once a social malaise and personal, moral failure. The pagan institutions of kinship, comitatus, wergeld, and peace-bond marriage are seen in every instance as inadequate to the menaces of ambition and blood-lust that threaten civilization. The vision is ideological, and while it presents the pagan past with a certain admiration and recognition that the struggle for good existed then, too, it is uncompromisingly Christian in perceiving the failure of pagan society as inevitable and complete.

Such a structure, while it may be called allegorical, is not, however, specifically theological in its allegory or intent. While clearly borrowing from exegetical tradition and founded on a Christian scheme of values it teaches no theological lessons. Seen in this way, *Beowulf* is a poem about society and history, and the poet adopts a structure suited to his theme that can be called allegorical to the extent that in the poem events in time have another meaning that transcends time; historical event and historical persons signify something as history and are real on that level, but they mean something more, without contradicting their literal sense, on a transhistoric level. In such an allegory Cain, for instance, with whom human history began, is a character of Genesis who was the first murderer and who was himself murdered in the seventh generation. But he is also his own descendant, Grendel, inasmuch as the monster signifies enmity towards peace and kinship in his role as a cannibal and a feuder who ravishes Heorot.[4] And he is Unferth as Unferth is his representative, who has murdered his brother and attempts to prevent Beowulf from ridding Heorot of the monster. Nevertheless both Grendel and Unferth have their own real existences, and so does Cain; they are not symbols of something else.

John Gardner in an admirable study of early medieval allegory generally describes the technique inherent in *Beowulf*:

In this allegorical technique Anglo-Saxon poets found a new means of expression. Instead of versifying Scriptural material, they could now explore secular images and situations in Christian terms. They had ready at hand virtually all the necessary stylistic devices for the writing of a poem like *Beowulf* – the Caedmonic device of rhythmic encoding, which could establish symbolic connections between events, and the techniques of vertical allegory which could turn Grendel, Grendel's mother, and the dragon into Christian-Platonic symbols of disorder.[5]

The term 'vertical allegory' is certainly good enough, but its main function here must be to distinguish the allegory of *Beowulf* from the allegory of Scripture, or christological allegory, as Gardner calls it.[6] In such a view *Beowulf* does not represent Christ or Abraham – nor Hrothgar, Moses – in a formal way, although he may suggest characteristics of these figures. As has been frequently pointed out, the necessary correspondences are not to be found, and the tone of the poem certainly seems to resist such a formal allegorical pattern. If instead allegory can be taken as saying one thing to mean many other things, *Beowulf* may be seen as allegorical.

The necessity of seeing in *Beowulf* a clear condemnation of paganism and all pagans in order to relate it to its historical Christian context seems somewhat exaggerated. Surely *Beowulf* is not peopled with evil characters without exception. To assert that the polemics and dogma of the eighth-and ninth-century theologian were known and adhered to by all those who could write and scrupulously reiterated in their writings seems an unnecessary extension of a general truth. As Robert Hanning has pointed out, the early Christians' usual attitude towards their past is shown in their total embrace of Rome. They favoured its continued dominance of the world and pointed out how much better a civilization it was since their arrival in it.[7]

The melancholy warmth shown by our poet towards certain institutions and traditions of the Germanic pagans may be due to much the same tendency. Rather than showing how much better such a civilization is since the arrival of the Christians, he has chosen the inverse proposition and shows us and his original audience how much worse it was before. Many of the so-called inconsistencies of attitude towards the past in the poem may reflect the somewhat paradoxical Christian attitude towards past history.

The examination of *Beowulf* from the perspective of the traditions of Cain evokes a panorama of social disaster characterized by parricide and the ravages of vengeance, and alleviated only by the actions of the morally heroic figures of the poem. To be sure, the poem speaks of several other things and suggests themes and images unrelated to the Cain tradition, but the present discussion has attempted to delineate the central theme of historical violence and transhistorical peace as well as its allegorical vocabulary. From the purely historical point of view it is perhaps not surprising that such a theme would inspire a poet of the time of the composition of *Beowulf*, considering the nature of social events of his contemporary and past history. Few dynasties of the various Germanic nations were unblemished by parricide and regicide, and all were marked by the ferocious struggle for wealth and power. The theme may well have been inspired by historical event. The meaning of that theme in the wider considerations of the human social condition and the nature of time as history would likely have been provided by the ideologial climate of which the poet was himself a product. To the Christian eye such a condition in pagan nations appeared as further proof of the ethical and spiritual flaws of those societies, but its persistence in newly converted states required an explanation that recognized the continuity, rather than the particularity, of this evil spirit. Such an explanation was found in the exegetical tradition of Cain, and the poetic use of this idea in *Beowulf* is expressed an an allegorical concept of time and civilization.

Complementary to the idea of evil's continuity in this perspective is the concomitant idea of the continuity of good. In the contemporary Christian society of the poet one witnesses the triumph of the 'right' ideology over the 'wrong' through the conversion of Britain or the world from paganism to Christianity; but one nevertheless admits the persistence of wrongness in some form. Similarly in such an allegorical vision of time the pagan past, while marked by the predominance of the 'wrong,' certainly must be seen to have continued within it some form of the right.

It does not, however, follow that precise correspondence must exist in poetic allegory in the form of prefigurations. That is not what the allegory of *Beowulf* is like; nor, for that matter, is it in that way that any of the most memorable medieval literary allegory functions. Rather it is in the nature of the poet's concept of time and the world that the allegory is constituted, since in this concept both the world and its historical dimension are symbolic realities.

The author of *Beowulf* is, then, both propagandist and poet simultaneously. His role as propagandist involves him in an attitude towards the present and future while his attitude towards the past is shaped by his role as poet. Although these two functions cannot be separated, except to explain them, we may easily contrast the phenomenon of the pure propagandist treating a similar theme. St Augustine, as author of *The City of God*, is a Christian propagandist delineating and defending an ideology in the present and for the future by contrast to the past. His attitude towards the past in this work is thus determined by the requirements of the function he assumes, and it is negative. The poetic process is otherwise. The

Beowulf poet, too, wishes to speak about the present and the future, but his function as poet leads him to memorialize the past. In the dynamics of his allegory the future is already demonstrated in the past, and he is therefore able, through a poetic reconstruction of the past, to speak about the future.

In his investigation of the nature of allegory, Angus Fletcher has related this mode to the poetic act of monumentalizing: 'The effect of monumentality remains constant, even in the vision of evil. Some predominant cultural ideal needs to be memorialized or publicly praised, and when the Renaissance poets make what they call "history" their model of moral instruction, they look to conflicts from which they can extract a "triumph"; they single out those moments of heroic behavior that can rightly become the monuments to a cultural ideal.'[8] It is perhaps less difficult to understand the eighth-century Christian poet's possible attitude towards his pagan past if we see it somewhat as Fletcher has described that of the Renaissance poet, who views historic event as material to be used for the memorializing of the past in order to monumentalize a cultural ideal of the present. Thus the scene of Beowulf's death and Wiglaf's prophecy, while providing a conclusion to the action of the poem, contains, as well, a vision of future time and civilization in which the struggle of good and evil represented in the past through Beowulf, Hrothgar, Grendel, and the dragon continues through time as history with varying climaxes of triumph and defeat. Such poetic allegory requires a reverent attitude towards the past, for what renders the future hopeful is that it is a fulfilment of the positive nature of time itself in its past mode.

The past, therefore, as presented in poetic allegory can never be unmitigatedly evil, for allegory cannot thus function. Time as an allegorical concept may never be constituted by one of its modes only – for instance, the present – to the exclusion of its others, in this case the past and the future. Instead time is presented as a whole, and while a given narrative may describe one or another mode primarily, the reality of the other modes is present through the allegorical structure of the work. The unity of such a time concept has to do not only with past, present, and future but also with the qualitative character of time: good and evil are not completely separable in time – the moment of good in the future, that of evil in the past – except in purely polemical writing. Continuity becomes the salient characteristic of such a temporal scheme, complemented by an eschatlogical direction.

Thus in *Beowulf* the hero is a pagan, probably a fictional one, who manifests some values ultimately to be condemned. Indeed, in one case he participates in one of the chief evils of the poem – vengeance. But he nevertheless represents the force of good, which on the one hand transcends the mores of a given social moment to become the spirit of a good society in abstraction, and which on the other hand will evolve in time to become the ethical code of a particular historical society dedicated to the principles of goodness. Thus the Christians, the particular historical society presumably dedicated to the principles of goodness, condemned polygamy in their own time but recognized that Abraham, a polygamist, represented the spirit of moral civilization that they would fulfil.

Beowulf simultaneously anticipates and represents higher social values than those held by his society because he possesses, at least by the end of the poem, a vision of history and its moral dynamics. This is not to suggest a relativity of values in the middle ages or on the part of the *Beowulf* poet. *Beowulf* is squarely set in its historical context, and by reference to that context it is immediately clear who is evil and who is good, who participates – however imperfectly – in history as an allegorical reality and who is enslaved in time as a material process.

The allegorical vision of *Beowulf* is one in which the poet's audience perceives itself as participating simultaneously in temporal and transtemporal reality. The didactic force of the poem is to emphasize that societies of the past have chosen to ignore the transtemporal in embracing the temporal alone through wrath, lust for power, and wealth, and that this same choice exists for present society. Beyond its didactic purpose, *Beowulf* sets forth the human predicament in social terms and relates it to the allegorical nature of history itself, or the story of man in time. Through the device of the exegetical tradition of Cain and the monsters, the development of civilization from the first moment of post-lapserian society to the Anglo-Saxon poem's contemporary moment is seen as an ordered and meaningful process in time, containing within it an eschatological reality gradually revealed. The allegorical mode reasserts that eschatological reality as the goal of civilization and history recalls the dilemma of man's freedom to choose to pursue the goal or not.

Notes

1 Goldsmith *Mode and Meaning*; Donahue '*Beowulf*, Ireland and the Natural Good,' and '*Beowulf* and Christian Tradition.' See, as well, Whallon and
  others 'Allegory, Tropology, or Neither.'
2 Goldsmith *Mode and Meaning* 70
3 Ibid 263
4 Fletcher *Allegory* 4
5 See Chadwick *The Growth of Literature* 1:556; also Donahue '*Beowulf* and
  Christian Tradition' who attempts to supply the liberal theological tradition
  that Chadwick requires. It might be observed that Donahue deforms the
  problem in his restatement of it when he says that Chadwick's objection that
  there was no liberal theological view of the pagan past must be answered
  before 'a cautious historian can be expected to take *Beowulf* in Tolkein's
  interpretation seriously as historical evidence for an eight-century Christian
  view of the Germanic pre-Christian past' (58). Thus posed, the problem is a
  historical one and ceases to be a literary problem capable of literary investigation.
6 Goldsmith *Mode and Meaning* 17–19
7 Jolliffe *Constitutional History of Medieval England* 2–3
8 Despite early Christians' theoretical objection to vengeance, Christianity historically entertained an ambiguous tolerance of the practice, and vengeance
  persists for a long while in Christianized societies. Although consistently
  discouraged, when the practice could be associated with the idea of 'just
  cause' it was not condemned, but it is exactly this qualitative concept of
  justice as opposed to the quantitative one of loss and restitution that the
  Christians found lacking in the pagan spirit. It is interesting to note that in the

matter of ordeals the Christians continued and expanded the Germanic practice, except for the one ordeal they opposed – the duel, the only one in which the parties physically assaulted one another.

9 Bede *Penetential of Theodore* 180. 'Si per iram [hominem occiderit], III annos; si casu, I. annum; si per poculum vel artem aliquam IIII annos aut plus; si per rixam X. annos peniteat.'

10 Pollock and Maitland *The History of English Law before the Time of Edward* I 1:46

11 See, for example, Goldsmith 'The Christian Theme of *Beowulf* '; Donahue 'Grendel and the Clanna Cain'; Hamilton 'The Religious Principle in *Beowulf* '; Bandy 'Cain, Grendel, and the Giants of *Beowulf.*' The fullest catalogue of the uses of the Cain legend in medieval literature remains Emerson 'Legends of Cain.'

12 Anderson *The Anglo-Saxon Scop* 17

13 Bede, Letter to Egbert, in *Baedae opera historica* 1:405–23

14 Anderson *Anglo-Saxon Scop* 35

15 Ibid (*Elene* 337)

16 Albertson *Anglo-Saxon Saints and Heroes* 21

17 William of Malmesbury *Gesta pontificum anglorum* 336. 'Ideo sanctum virum, super pontem qui rura et urbem continuat, abeuntibus se opposuisse obicem, quasi artem cantitandi professum. Eo plusquam semel facto, plebis favorem et concursum emeritum. Hoc commento sensim inter ludicra verbis Scripturarum insertis, cives ad sanitatem reduxisse.'

18 Ibid 334. 'Ad pedes Adriani, qui esset fons litterarum.'

19 Aldhelm's warning to Wihtfrid about the seductive powers of classical myth can hardly be taken as a refutation of his interest in secular literature. It is noteworthy that Aldhelm does not include in his condemnations Irish or Anglo-Saxon literary legends.

20 William of Malmesbury *Gesta pontificum anglorum* 336. 'Litteris itaque ad plenum instructus, nativae quoque linguae non negligebat camina; adeo ut, teste libro Elfredi, de quo superius dixi, nulla umquam aetate par ei fuerit quisquam. Poesim Anglicam posse facere, cantum componere, eadem apposite vel cantere vel dicere.'

21 See Duckett *Anglo-Saxon Saints and Scholars* 33f

22 Whallon *Formula, Character, and Context* 117. Whallon, however, concludes through analysis of formulaic patterns that the poem is a product more of its pagan past than of its Christian present.

23 Bede *Opera historica* 1:lii (note)

24 Bede *In Genesin* 2:ix, 4. 'Ferunt autem quod in hoc maxima fuerit praeuaricatio gigantum, quia cum sanguine carnem comederent; ideoque Dominus,

illis diluuio exstrinctis, carne quidem uesci homines concesserit, sed ne id cum sanguine facerent prohibuerit.'
25 Faricio *Vita S. Aldhelmi* 66. 'Prophetarum exempla, Davidis psalmos, Salomonis tria volumina, Hebraicis litteris bene novit, et legem Mosaicam.'
26 See Sutcliffe 'The Venerable Bede's Knowledge of Hebrew.'
27 Augustine 'On Nature and Grace' 550
28 Tertullian *De patientia* 5, in *Opera* 3:8
29 Chrysostom *Homily 24* on 2 Corinthians 2:12, PG 61:568
30 Rupertus *De victoria verbi dei* 2, PL 169:1258. 'Primum serpentis semen existit Cain. Hinc Joannes in Epistola sua: "Non, inquit, sicut Cain, qui ex maligno erat (I Joan. iii)," serpentis ergo semen erat videlicet imitatione invidiae, non natura.'

CHAPTER 2: THE CAIN TRADITION

1 *Bibliotheca Rabbinica* 1:290. 'An Angel was destined to be their origin [the posterity of Cain], who, attracted by the beauty of Eve, entered her riding upon a serpent, whence Cain was conceived whose appearance and that of his posterity was not human but angelic / Primus eorum parens affignatur angelus qui pulchritudine Evae illectus, equitans super serpentem ad eam ingreditur, ex quo concepit Kaim, cuius figuram ut et illius posteritatis, non humanam, sed angelicam fuisse autumant.'
2 Goldsmith *Mode and Meaning* 105
3 Tertullian's description in *De patientia* of Eve pregnant with the evil of Satan is one example of how the image survived: *Opera* 3:8.
4 An example of such a development of the tradition is seen in Rupertus *De victoria verbi dei* 2, PL 169:1260.
5 See, for example, Angelomus *Commentarius in Genesim* PL 115:146.
6 See, for example, Ambrose *De Cain et Abel* CSEL 32:341.
7 See, for example, Commodianus *Instructiones* 1, iii, in *Instructions of Commodian* trans. R.E. Wallace ANCL 18:435. On cannibalism in particular, see, for example, Clement *Homily 8*, in *Clementine Homilies* ANCL 17:144.
8 See, for example, Aelfric *Interrogationes Sigewulfi in Genesin* in *Anglia* 7:10.
9 *The Apochrypha and Pseudepigrapha of the Old Testament in English* ed R.H. Charles (Oxford, Clarendon Press 1913)
10 *Josephus* 4:25, 27
11 Ibid 4:25
12 Ibid 4:29
13 Bede and Aldhelm, for example, demonstrate a wide knowledge of the *Georgics*. See Ogilvy *Books known to Anglo-Norman Writers* 258.

14 *Georgics* I, 125f. See also Ovid *Fasti* I, 135f. This too seems to have been known to Aldhelm (Ogilvy *Books known to Anglo-Norman Writers* 212).

15 This is the original Talmudic idea. See, for example, Polano *Selections from the Talmud* 29.

16 See, for example, Aelfric's *Interrogationes Sigewulfi* 9.

17 See, for example, Philo *Confusion of Tongues* in *Works* 4:77.

18 'From this arose jealousy and envy, strife and sedition, persecution and disorder, as well as war and captivity. / Ex hoc zelus et invidia, et contentio et contumacia, et persecutio et inconstantia, et proelium et captivitas.' *Clementis ad Corinthios* 3:2–4, in *Florilegium Patristicum* 44:9–11

19 See, for example, Rupertus *De victoria verbi dei* 2, PL 169:1258.

20 St John Chrysostom in the fourth century emphasized the uniqueness of Cain's act: 'For, as in the case of Cain, what was done was not a murder only, but worse than even many murders; for it was not a stranger, but a brother whom he slew, and a brother who had not done, but suffered wrong; not after many murders, but having first originated the horrid crime. / 'Quaemadmodum enim Caini crimen non caedes modo erat, sed multis caedibus pejus; non enim alienum, sed fratrem; et fratrem, non laedentem, sed laesum occidit; non post multas patratas caedes, sed ipse exsecrandum scelus prior invenit.' *Homily* 26, PG 57:341

21 Ambrose *Praecationes duae* 2:4, PL 17:835. '"Invidia diaboli mors introivit in orbem terrarum" (Sap. II, 24). Cain persuasit ut livoris odio fraternum funderet sanguinem. Sed nimirum idem Cain invidus prius suam animam, quam alterius carnem peremit, scriptum quippe est: 'Qui odit fratrem suum, homicida est.'' (I Joan. III, 15).'

22 *Homily 3* in *The Homilies of Wulfstan* 145–6

23 This subject is more fully developed in my article 'The Exile as Uncreator.'

24 See, for example, Cyprianus Gallus *Genesis et Sodoma* 1538.

25 See, for example, Ambrose *De Cain et Abel* CSEL 32:408.

26 See, for example, Philo *Questions and Answers on Genesis* 1:76, in *Works: Supplement* 1:44–5.

27 Bede *In Genesin* in *Opera* 2:i, 78–9. 'Tertio ut in eadem terra uagas semper esset et profugus, neque ausus uspiam sedes habere quietas.'

28 Augustine *Contra Julianum* PL 45:1555. 'Cain vero fratricidae apparet omnibus immane peccatum, et scelus esse constat horrendum ... Et cum ille audiens terram non sibi daturam fructum secundum laborem suum, et super eam cum gemitu et tremore miserum se futurum, magis mortis formidine quateretur, ne quis ei faceret, quod ipse fecerat fratri.'

29 Among others, St Jerome expresses the interpretation in letter xxxvi, 2, in *Epistolae* CSEL 54:271.

30 See note 27.

31 Inter. 89, PL 100:525. 'Quod est signum Cain, quod posuit [ei] Deus, ut non occideretur (vers. 15) – Resp. Ipsum videlicet signum quod tremens et gemens, vagus et profugus semper viveret; nec audere eum uspiam orbis terrarum sedes habere quietas.'

32 *Commentariorum in Genesim* 2, PL 107:506–7: 'nec audere ... sedes habere quietas.'

33 See, for example, Remegius of Lyons *Commentarius in Genesim* PL 131:70. 'This is shown concerning them [the Jews] who throughout the whole Roman world are wanderers and exiles and have no permanent seat. / Hoc de eis manifestum est qui per omnem Romani orbis imperium vagi et profugi sunt nec usquam habent certas sedes.' See also Angelomus *Commentarius in Genesim* PL 115:151.

34 'Old Saxon Genesis' 45; translation in Emerson 863

35 Emerson 'Legends of Cain' 873

36 Jerome *Hebraicae Quaestiones in Libro Geneseos* CC 72:7: 'Naid transtulerunt, in hebraeo Nod dicitur, et interpretatur σδαενσηφσς id est instabilis et fluctuans ac sedis incertae.'

37 For example, Cyprian *Liber de Zelo et Livore* CSEL 3,1:426.

38 Ambrose *De Cain et Abel* CSEL 32:405. 'abscondit se autem qui uelare uult culpam et tegere peccatum. qui enim male agit odit lucem et tenebras suorum quaerit ut latibula delictorum.'

39 Ibid, 32: 408. 'reppulit enim eum a facie sua et a parentibus abdicatum separatae habitationis quodam relegauit exilio, eo quod ab humana mansuetudine transisset ad saeuitiam bestiarum.'

40 W.P. Patterson 'Cain' *Dictionary of the Bible* ed James Hastings (5 vols, Edinburgh 1910) vol 1, 338–9

41 Jerome *Commentariorum in Osee* 3, xi, PL 25:290. 'Possumus et aliter dicere: quia primus Cain parricida exstruxit civitatem in nomine filii sui Enoch, in hujuscemodi urbem Dominus non ingreditur, quae ex scelere et sanguine et parricideo fabricata est.'

42 Augustine *De civitate Dei* 4:426. 'Primus itaque fuit terrenea civitatis conditor fratricide; nam suam fratrem, civem civitatis alternae in hac terra peregrinantem, invidentia victus occidit.'

43 Philo claimed this to have been impossible and offered more exotic explanations. Augustine's authority was enough to decide the matter in favour of this more conventional solution, at least as far as orthodoxy was concerned: see *De Natura et Gratia* CSEL 60:265–6.

44 See, for example, Ambrose *De Cain et Abel* CSEL: 32:408.

45 Clement *Homily* 8 in *Clementine Homilies* ANCL 17:142–3

46 See, for example, Philo *The Worse attacks the Better* in *Works* 2:255.
47 See, for example, Theophilus *To Autolycus* in *Writings of Tatian and Theophilus* ed M. Dods, ANCL 3:95 (Edinburgh 1867).
48 See, for example, Justin Martyr *Apologia* 2 in *The Writings* 61.
49 *Josephus* 4:31: 'Jûbel [Tubal-Cain] one of the sons of the other wife, surpassing all men in strength, distinguished himself in the art of war, procuring also thereby the means for satisfying the pleasures of the body, and first invented the forging of metal.'
50 See Emerson 'Legends of Cain' 888–9.
51 See, for example, Isidore of Seville *Chronicon* PL 83:1020.
52 *Genesis* ASPR 1:47
53 For a summary of this tradition see Robert Graves and R. Patai *Hebrew Myths: Book of Genesis* (London 1965) 108–10.
54 See Lactantius *Divinae Institutiones* in *Opera* CSEL 19,i:163–4.
55 Augustine *De civitate Dei* 4:552–3. 'Potuerunt igitur gigantes nasci et prius quam filii Dei, qui et angeli Dei dicti sunt, filiabus hominum, hoc est secundum hominem viventium, miscerentur, filii scilicet Seth filiis Cain.'
56 Augustine *Quaestionum in Heptateuchum* 1 iii, CSEL 28:5
57 Anselm of Laon (eleventh century): 'for even after the Flood there existed not only men, but women of huge stature. / 'post diluvium corpora non solum virorum, sed et mulierum incredibilii magnitudine existerunt.'
58 For example, Gregory *Moralium* PL 76:24–5
59 See *Beowulf and the Fight at Finnsburg* Introduction xxi, note 7.
60 Alcuin, Inter 96, *Interrogationes et Responsiones in Genesin* PL 100:526. 'De quibus dixit: ''Cum coepissent homines multiplicari super terram et filias procreassent ...'' Resp. Filias hominum, progeniem Cham; et fillios Dei sobolem Seth [ms: Sem] appellare Scriptura voluit. Hi avita benedictione religiosi; illae paterna maledictione impudiciae [ms: illi ... impudici]: sed postquam filii Seth [ms: Sem] concupiscentia victi ex filiabus Cham connubia junxerunt, ex tali conjunctione homines immenso corpore, viribus superbi, moribus [inconditi], quos Scriptura gigantes nominat procreati sunt.'
61 See Aelfic *Old English Version of the Heptateuch* 99.
62 See, for example, Athenagoras *Apologia* 31–2.
63 See, for example. Boethius as rendered by Alfred: *De consolatione philosophiae* 3:12.
64 Emerson 'Legends of Cain' 883–4
65 Ambrose *De Noe et Arca* 34:128, CSEL 32:496–7. 'Nembroth autem per interpretationem Aethiops dicitur. color Aethiopis tenebras animae squaloremque significat, qui aduersus lumini est, claritatis exors, tenebris inuolutus,

nocti similior quam diei. uenatoris quoque usus in siluis, inter feras ac bestias conuersatio eius.' See also Philastrius *Liber de Haeresibus* PL 12:1224.

66 See Augustine *Quaestionum in Heptateuchum* 5, iii. Also *Liber de situ et nominibus: De Libro Jesu* PL 23:914.

67 See, for example, *Josephus* 4:31

68 Peter Comestor calls him 'manzer' – 'illegitimate,' 'bastard,' 'unclean' (*Historia scholastica* PL 198:1311)

69 Philo *Confusion of Tongues* in *Works* 4:77

70 See, for example, *Homily* 8 in *Clementine Homilies* ANCL 17:142.

71 Justin Martyr *Second Apology* in *The Writings* 75–6

72 Emerson 'Legends of Cain' 905

73 Cassian *Second Conference of Abbot Serenus* in *Les Conférences* 30–1. 'Haec igitur quam diximus curiosarum rerum notitia quomodo in diluuio non perierit ac superuenientibus saeculis innotuerit ... Quantum itaque traditiones ferunt, Cham filius Noe, qui superstitionibus istis et sacrilegis ac profanis erat artibus institutus, sciens nullum se posse super his memorialem librum in arcam prorsus inferre, in qua erat una cum patre iusto ac sanctis fratribus ingressurus, scelestas artes ac profana commenta diuersorum metallorum lamminis, quae scilicet aquarum conrumpi inundatione non passent, et durissimis lapidibus insculpsit. Quae peracto diluuio eadem qua celauerat curiositate perquirens sacrilegiorum ac perpetuae nequitiae seminarium transmisit in posteros ... De illis ergo quemadmodum diximus filiis Seth et filiabus Cain nequiores filii procreati sunt, qui fuerunt robustissimi venatores, violentissimi ac truculentissimi viri qui pro inormitate corporum vel crudelitatis atque malitiae gigantes sunt.'

74 Carney *Studies in Irish Literature and History*

75 Ibid 102, note 1

76 Clement *Homily* 8

77 Gregory *Moralium* 20:39, PL: 76:183. ' "Frater fui draconum, et socius struthionum ..." Quid draconum nomine nisi malitiosorum hominum vita signatur? ... Abel quippe esse renuit, quem Cain malitia non exercet.'

78 There is a more modest but parallel tradition of the good dragon, as indeed there is of the good giant. The salient feature of the good dragon is, significantly, that he protects the city.

79 In Renaissance art a dragon pulls the chariot of Saturn, the realist culmination of an older aesthetic tradition.

80 It is perhaps significant that in ancient medicine these three elements are components in cures for physical disorders.

81 The killing of the dragon always signifies the taming of wildness. The more

psychological form is found in the marrying of the woman, frequent symbol of disorder in the middle ages, to the conqueror. Another version is seen in the story of Perceval, who rescues a lion cub from a dragon, producing the immediate and complete taming of its ferocious parent. Lions are often pitted, literally and symbolically, against dragons, as in the story of Daniel.

82 Gregory *Moralium* 34:38, PL 76:716. '[Leviathan] Invidiae quoque flamma Cain animum succendit, cum de accepto fratris sacrificio doluit, et per hoc usque ad fratricidii facinus pervenit.'

CHAPTER 3: THE POETIC PRESENT AND THE FABULOUS MODE

1 See also Tennenhouse '*Beowulf* and the Sense of History.'
2 Goldsmith *Mode and Meaning* 83
3 So Klaeber would lead us to believe: 'In fact, it almost looks as if Hroðulf were conceived of as a sort of joint-regent in Denmark.' *Beowulf and the Fight at Finnsburg* Introduction xxxii.
4 Goldsmith *Mode and Meaning* 83
5 See, for example, Cotton Claudius B IV, f 13r, eds Rosenkilde and Bagger, in *Old English Illustrated Heptateuch*, vol 18 of *Early English Manuscripts in Facsimile* eds C.R. Dodwell, Peter Clemoes et al (Copenhagen 1974).
6 Cyprian *Liber de Zelo et Livore* CSEL 3,i:426. 'in tenebris ambulat.'
7 Ambrose *De Cain et Abel* CSEL 32:405. 'odit lucem et tenebras suorum quaerit'
8 C.L. Wrenn *Beowulf with the Finnesburg Fragment* (London 1953) 188–9, note to lines 168–9.
9 See also Chaney 'Grendel and the Gifstol.'
10 *Liber Monstrorum* 71. 'Et quaedam insula in Orientalibus orbis terrarum partibus esse dicitur, in qua nascuntur homines rationabili statura, nisi quod eorum oculi sicut lucernae lucent.'
11 Peter Comestor *Verbum abbreviatum* PL 205:387
12 Basil *The Letters* 4:55–7
13 Lines 161–2: 'Sinnihte heold / mistige moras'; lines 1357–8: 'Hie dygel lond / warigeað wulfhleoþu'
14 See note 39, chapter 2.
15 For a more allegorical interpretation of the mere, see Robertson 'The Doctrine of Charity.'
16 The English sense of the verb 'to nod,' meaning to shake one's head in assent, may be derived from a combination of Cain's place of exile, Nod in English, and his sign, a spastic shaking of head and limbs.
17 Clarke *Sidelights on Teutonic History* 244f
18 Clébert *Dictionnaire* 166

19 For a discussion of the treasure in *Beowulf* from a similar point of view, see Condren '*Unnyt* Gold in *Beowulf* 3168.'
20 Cherniss *Ingeld and Christ* chapter 4
21 Whitelock *The Beginnings of English Society* 30–1
22 Gardner *The Construction of Poetry in Old English* 34. It should be pointed out, however, that Gardner, too, sees Beowulf as a tragically flawed hero.
23 The manuscript is unclear. I prefer, with W.W. Lawrence, the reading 'þegn.' The fact that the thief seeks his own means of compounding the dispute, rather than having the means supplied by a master, encourages acceptance of Lawrence's reading of 'thane,' to whom the law would have allowed such initiative. No slave would have been permitted to accomplish wergeld on his own. See Helder 'Beowulf and the Plundered Hoard.'
24 Lawrence *Beowulf and the Epic Tradition* 56
25 Seebohm *Tribal Customs in Anglo-Saxon Law* 17
26 Augustine *De civitate Dei* 15:5
27 Philo *Confusion of Tongues* in *Works* 4:77
28 Goldsmith *Mode and Meaning* 155
29 Ibid 222
30 Ibid 224
31 Goldsmith 'The Christian Perspective in *Beowulf*' 83
32 If 'stanbogan' is left as subject and 'eorðreced' object (as opposed to Klaeber's suggestion) we have a picture of this earth hall, or burial mound, existing within the arches and columns of an ancient ruined city. The burial mound might have been constructed after the fall of the city.

CHAPTER 4: THE DIGRESSIONS: PAST THROUGH ALLUSION, FUTURE THROUGH PROPHECY

1 Chambers *Beowulf: An Introduction* 90–1
2 See Kaske 'The Sigemund-Heremod and Hama-Hygelac Passages in *Beowulf*.'
3 Elton and Powell *Saxo Grammaticus* 15f
4 Blake 'The Heremod Digressions in *Beowulf*' 285
5 See also Lee *The Guest-Hall of Eden*.
6 Kaske 'The *Eotenas* in *Beowulf*' 289
7 The *e* of 'eotena' is written here exactly as in other uses of the word in the manuscript. Klaeber's capitalization of it (lines 902, 1072, 1088, 1141, 1145) grows directly out of an interpretation of the word as 'Jute.' If the present reading is correct, 'eoten' would not be capitalized in any of the instances in the poem.

8 In reference to the Germanic practice of 'ring giving,' this last would seem tantamount to an effort to include the Danes in the Frisian kin.

9 Lawrence *Beowulf and the Epic Tradition* 390f.

10 I take 'agan' in the sense of 'restore,' 'give,' or 'provide,' and 'geweald' in the sense of 'power as protection.'

11 I prefer with Wrenn and others to retain the original manuscript reading of line 1141 as 'inne' instead of Klaeber's emendation 'irne,' and in 1142 the original 'worold rædenne' instead of Klaeber's 'w(e)orodrædende.' I take the word 'rædenne' as accusative singular of 'ræden,' meaning 'condition,' 'direction.' 'World direction' or 'world condition' would seem to carry the sense of 'the way things go in the world.' I believe the poet may be alluding in this context to the ethics prevalent in a society when he uses the word 'woroldrædenne,' and specifically referring to the pagan ethic of vengeance. The most colloquial translation of the word would be 'the way of the world.'

12 For example, see Burchard of Worms *Decretum* 952–4.

13 We are speaking here, of course, not of the laws in force in the heathen continental society of Haethcyn's own time but of those of the poet's time, as an indication of the mental disposition of the poet's English audience.

14 Klaeber *Beowulf and the Fight at Finnsburg* 177–8, note to lines 1197–1201

15 Brodeur *The Art of Beowulf* 177

16 Klaeber *Beowulf and the Fight at Finnsburg* Introduction xxxv

17 Lee *Guest Hall of Eden* 121

18 Malone 'Hrethric' 285

19 Brodeur *The Art of Beowulf* 142–6

20 Ibid 156

21 Sisam *The Structure of Beowulf* 38

22 Bonjour *The Digressions in Beowulf* 38

CHAPTER 5: CONCLUSION

1 Hamilton 'Religious Principle in *Beowulf*' 314

2 Ibid 329

3 Ibid

4 Similarly Grendel's dam may be seen as an Eve figure, the origin of evil progeny, and the dragon a monstrous form of Satan.

5 Gardner *The Construction of Poetry in Old English* 52–3

6 Ibid 59

7 Hanning *The Vision of History in Early Britain* 22

8 Fletcher *Allegory* 361

Bibliography

This bibliography lists only those works cited in the text. The following abbreviations are used.

ANCL Ante-Nicene Christian Library
ASPR Anglo-Saxon Poetic Records
CC Corpus Christianorum series latina
CSEL Corpus scriptorum ecclesiasticorum latinorum
EETS Early English Text Society
MGH Monumenta Germaniae Historica
PG Patrologiae cursus completus: Series graeca
PL Patrologiae cursus completus: Series latina
PMLA *Publications of the Modern Language Association*

PRIMARY WORKS

Aelfric 'Aelfric's Version of *Alcuini Interrogationes Sigewulfi in Genesin*'
  edited by G.E. McLean in *Anglia* 7 (1884) 1–59
– *De Veteri et Novo Testamento* edited by S.J. Crawford in *The Old English
  Version of the Heptateuch* EETS 160 (London 1922)
Alcuin *Beati Flacci Albini seu Alcuini Abbatis Epistolae* Cura ac Studio Fro-
  benii, S.R.I., Principis Abbatis as S. Emmeramum (Ratisbonae 1717)
– *Interrogationes et Responsiones in Genesin* PL 100: 515–68
– *Letter to Ethelred*, circa 795, edited by A.W. Haddan and William Stubbs in
  Councils and Ecclesiastical Documents Relating to England and Ireland
  (3 vols, Oxford 1869–78) vol 3

Alfred [King] *Laws* edited by Benjamin Thorpe in *Ancient Laws and Institutes of England* (London 1840)
- *De Consolatione Philosophiae: King Alfred's Old English Version* edited by W.J. Sedgefield (Oxford 1900)
Ambrose [Saint] *De Cain et Abel* edited by Carolus Schenkl in *Opera* pars 1, CSEL 32 (Vindobonae 1897)
- *De Noe et Arca* edited by Carolus Schenkl in *Opera* pars 1, CSEL 32 (Vindobonae 1897)
- *Enarrationes in Psalmos* edited by M. Petschenig in *Opera* pars 6, CSEL 64 (Vindobonae 1919)
- *Expositio Apocalypsis* PL 17: 765–970
- *Epistulae et Acta* edited by Otto Faller SI, in *Opera*; CSEL 82 (Vindobonae 1968)
- *Praecationes Duae* [Ambrose?] PL 17: 829–42
Anselm of Laon. *Glossa Ordinaria: Liber Genesis* PL 113: 67–182
Athenagoras *Apologia* edited and translated by J.A. Giles in *Writings of the Early Christians of the Second Century* (London 1857)
Augustine [Saint] *De Civitate Dei* edited by G.E. McCraken and others. Loeb classical Library (7 vols, Cambridge, Mass, and London 1957–)
- *Contra Julianum* PL 45: 1049–1608
- *Epistolae* edited by A. Goldbacher, CSEL 34 (Vindobonae 1895), CSEL 44 (1904), CSEL 57 (1911), CSEL 58 (1911)
- *Enarrationes in Psalmos* edited by D.B. Dekkers and J. Fraipont, CC 38, pars 10, i; 39, pars 10, 2; 40, pars 10, 3 (Turnholti 1956)
- *Commentaire de la première épître de Saint Jean* edited by Paul Agaesse SJ (Paris 1961)
- *De Natura et gratia* edited by C.F. Urba and J. Zycha, CSEL 60 (Vindobonae 1913)
- *Quaestionum in Heptateuchum* edited by J. Zycha, CSEL 28 (Vindobonae 1894)
- 'On Nature and Grace' in *Basic Writings of St. Augustine* edited by Whitney J. Oates (2 vols, New York 1948) vol 1
Basil [Saint] *The Letters* edited by Roy Deferrari. Loeb Classical Library (4 vols, Cambridge Mass, and London 1926–34)
Bede [Venerable] *In Genesin* edited by C.W. Jones in *Opera*, CC 118a, pars 2, i (Turnholti 1967)
- *Penitential* edited by A.W. Haddan and William Stubbs in *Councils and Ecclesiastical Documents Relating to England and Ireland* (3 vols, Oxford 1869–78) vol 3
- *Baedae Opera historica* edited by Charles Plummer (2 vols; Oxford 1896)
- *Second Conference of Augustine's Oak*, AD 603, edited by A.W. Haddan

and William Stubbs in *Councils and Ecclesiastical Documents Relating to England and Ireland* (3 vols, Oxford 1869–78) vol 1

Beowulf and the Fight at Finnsburg edited by Frederick Klaeber (3rd ed, Boston 1941)

Bibliotheca Rabbinica edited by Julius Bartolocci (Rome 1675)

Burchard of Worms *Decretum* PL 140: 943–1014

Cassian *Les Conférences* edited by Dom E. Pichery in *Sources chrétiennes* 54 (Paris 1958)

Chrysostom [Saint] John *Homily* 7 PG 61: 441–54; *Homily* 24, PG 61: 563–70; *Homily* 26, PG 57: 333–44; *Homily* 86, PG 58: 763–70

Clement [Saint] *S. Clementis Romani Epistula ad Corinthios* edited by Carolus T. Schaefer in *Florilegium Patristicum* 44 (Bonn 1941)

– *Clementine Homilies* translated by the Rev. Thomas Smith, ANCL 17 (Edinburgh 1870)

– *Die Pseudoklementinen* II: *Rekognitionen* edited by Bernard Rehm and Fr. Pasche in *Griechischen Christlichen Schriftsteller* 51 (Berlin 1965)

Cyprian [Saint] *Liber de Zelo et Livore* edited by G. Hartel in *Opera*, CSEL 3, 1 (Vindobonae 1868)

Cyprianus Gallus *Genesis et Sodoma* in *Opera et Fragmenta Veterum Poetarum Latinorum* edited by Michael Mettaire (2 vols, London J. Nicholson 1713)

Faricio *Vita S. Aldhelmi Faricio Auctore*, PL 89: 63–84

'Genesis' edited by G.P. Krapp in *The Junius Manuscript* ASPR 1 (New York 1931)

Gregory I [Saint] *Moralium*, PL 75: 515–1162, PL 76: 10–782

Jerome [Saint] *Commentariorum in Esaiam* edited by Marc Adriaen in *Opera* pars 1, *Opera Exegetica* 2, CC 73 (Turnholti 1963)

– *Commentariorum in Osee*, PL 25: 809–946

– *Epistolae* edited by I. Hilberg, CSEL 54, pars 1, i (Vindobonae 1910)

– *Hebraicae Quaestiones in Libro Geneseos* edited by P. Antin OSB, in *Opera* pars 1, *Opera Exegetica* 1, CC 62 (Turnholti 1959)

– *Liber de Situ et Nominibus*, PL 23: 903–76

Josephus, Flavius *Jewish Antiquities* in *Josephus* 4, edited by H.St.-J. Thackery. Loeb Classical Library (9 vols, Cambridge, Mass, and London 1967)

Justin Martyr *The Writings of Justin Martyr and Athenagorus* translated by Marcus Dods and B.P. Pratten; ANCL (Edinburgh 1867)

Lactantius *Divinae Institutiones* edited by Samuel Brandt and G. Laubmann in *Opera*, CSEL 19 i (Vindobonae 1890)

Liber Monstrorum edited by D. Butturff in 'Monsters and the Scholar: An Edition and Critical Study of the Liber Monstrorum' (PH D dissertation, University of Illinois 1968)

Liber Monstrorum et Liber de Belluis edited by Jules Berger de Xivrey in *Traditions Tératologiques* (Paris 1836)

'Old Saxon Genesis' edited by R. Zangemeister and W. Braune in *Altsachsische Bibeldichtung* (Heidelberg 1894)

Philastrius *Liber de Haeresibus* PL 12: 1049–1302

Philo [Judaeus] *Works* edited and translated by F.H. Colson and G.H. Whitaker. Loeb Classical Library (5 vols, Cambridge, Mass, and London 1937–56)

Rabanus Maurus *Commentariorum in Genesim* PL 107: 439–668

– *Enarrationum in Librum Numerorum* PL 108: 587–836

The Talmud edited and translated by H. Polano in *Selections from the Talmud* (np 1876)

Tertullian *Adversus Judaeos* edited by A. Kroyman in *Opera* pars 2, CSEL 70 (Vindobonae 1942)

– *Adversus Marcionem* edited by A. Kroyman in *Opera* pars 3, CSEL 47 (Vindobonae 1906)

– *De Patientia* edited by A. Kroyman in *Opera* pars 3, CSEL 47 (Vindobonae 1906)

– *Liber de Praescriptionibus* edited by A. Kroyman in *Opera* pars 3, CSEL 47 (Vindobonae 1906)

Wulfstan *The Homilies of Wulfstan* edited by Dorothy Bethurum (Oxford 1957)

SECONDARY WORKS

Aldhelm *Opera* edited by Rudolph Ehwald, MGH: auct. ant. 15 (Berolini 1913–19)

Albertson, Clinton *Anglo-Saxon Saints and Heroes* (New York, Fordham University Press 1967)

Anderson, Lewis F. *The Anglo-Saxon Scop* University of Toronto Studies: Philological Series 1 (Toronto 1903)

Bandy, Stephen C. 'Cain, Grendel and the Giants of *Beowulf*' *Papers on Language and Literature* 9 (1973) 235–49

Blake, N.F. 'The Heremod Digressions in *Beowulf*' *Journal of English and Germanic Philology* 61 (1962) 278–87

Bonjour, Adrien *The Digressions in Beowulf* Medium Aevum Monograph 5 (Oxford 1950)

Brodeur, A.G. *The Art of Beowulf* (Berkeley 1959)

Carney, James *Studies in Irish Literature and History* (Dublin 1955)

Chadwick, H.M. *The Growth of Literature* 1 (Cambridge 1932)

Chambers, R.W. *Beowulf: An Introduction* (Cambridge 1959)

Chaney, William A. 'Grendel and the Gifstol: A Legal View of Monsters'; PMLA 78 (1962) 513–20

Cherniss Michael D. *Ingeld and Christ: Heroic Concepts and Values in Old English Poetry* (Mouton 1972)

Clarke, M.G. *Sidelights on Teutonic History during the Migration Period* Girton College Studies 3 (Cambridge 1911)

Clébert, J-P *Dictionnaire du symbolisme animal* (Paris 1971)

Condren, Edward '*Unnyt* Gold in *Beowulf* 3168' *Philological Quarterly* 52 (1973) 296–9

Davidson, H.R.E. *The Sword in Anglo-Saxon England* (Oxford 1962)

Donahue, Charles 'Grendel and the Clanna Cain' *Journal of Celtic Studies* 1 (1950) 167–75

– '*Beowulf*, Ireland and the Natural Good' *Traditio* 7 (1949–51) 236–77

– '*Beowulf* and Christian Tradition: A Reconsideration from a Celtic Stance' *Traditio* 21 (1965) 55–116

Duckett, Eleanor Shipley *Anglo-Saxon Saints and Scholars* (Hamden, Conn. 1967)

Elton, Oliver, and F.Y. Powell, eds. *The First Nine Books of Saxo Grammaticus* (London 1894)

Emerson, Oliver 'Legends of Cain, Especially in Old and Middle English' 21 (1906) 831–939

Fletcher, Angus *Allegory: The Theory of a Symbolic Mode* (Ithaca 1964)

Gardner, John *The Construction of Poetry in Old English* (Carbondale, Ill 1975)

Goldsmith, Margaret 'The Christian Theme of *Beowulf*' *Medium Aevum* 29 (1960) 81–101

– 'The Christian Perspective in *Beowulf*' *Comparative Literature* 14 (1962) 71–90

– *The Mode and Meaning of 'Beowulf'* (London 1970)

Hamilton, Marie Padgett 'The Religious Principle in *Beowulf*' PMLA 61 (1946) 309–31

Hanning, Robert W. *The Vision of History in Early Britain* (New York 1966)

Helder, Willem 'Beowulf and the Plundered Hoard' *Neuphilologische Mitteilungen* 4, 78 (1977) 317–25

Hodgkin, Thomas *Italy and Her Invaders* (8 vols, Oxford 1880)

Irving, Edward *A Reading of Beowulf* (New Haven 1968)

Jolliffe, J.E.A. *Constitutional History of Medieval England* (London 1967)

Kaske, R.E. '*Sapientia et Fortitudo* as the Controlling Theme of *Beowulf*' *Studies in Philology* 55 (1958) 423–57

– 'The Sigemund-Heremod and Hama-Hygelac Passages in *Beowulf*' PMLA 74 (1959) 489–94

– 'The *Eotenas* in *Beowulf*' in *Old English Poetry: Fifteen Essays* edited by Robert P. Creed (Providence 1967)

Lawrence, W.W. *Beowulf and the Epic Tradition* (Cambridge, Mass 1928)

Lee, A.A. *The Guest-Hall of Eden: Four Essays on the Design of Old English Poetry* (New Haven 1972)

Leyerle, John 'Beowulf the Hero and the King' *Medium Aevum* 34 (1965) 89–102

– 'The Interlace Structure of *Beowulf*' *University of Toronto Quarterly* 37 (1967) 1–17

Malone, Kemp 'Hrethric' PMLA 42 (1927) 268–313

– (ed) *Widsith* in *Anglistica* 13 (1962) 1–231

Mellinkoff, Ruth 'Cain's Monstrous Progeny in *Beowulf*: Part I, Noachic Tradition' *Anglo-Saxon England* 8 (1980) 143–62

Ogilvy, Jack *Books known to Anglo-Norman Writers from Aldhelm to Alcuin* (Cambridge, Mass, Medieval Academy of America 1936)

Pépin, Jean *Mythe et allégorie* (Paris, Aubier, 1958)

Pertz, G.H., (ed) MGH: *Leges* 1–5 (Hanover 1863–)

Pollock, Sir Frederick, and F.W. Maitland *The History of English Law before the Time of Edward* I (2 vols; London, Cambridge University Press 1968)

Robertson, D.W. 'The Doctrine of Charity in Medieval Literary Gardens,' *Speculum* 26 (1951) 24–49

Seebohm, Frederic *Tribal Customs in Anglo-Saxon Law* (London 1902)

Shapiro, Meyer 'Cain's Jaw-Bone that Did the First Murder' *Art Bulletin* 24 (1942) 205–12

Sisam, Kenneth *The Structure of Beowulf* (Oxford 1965)

Sutcliffe, E.F. 'The Venerable Bede's Knowledge of Hebrew' *Biblica* 16 (1935) 300–6

Tennenhouse, Leonard '*Beowulf* and the Sense of History' *Bucknell Review* 19, iii (1971) 137–46

Thorpe, Benjamin *Ancient Laws and Institutes of England* (2 vols, London 1840)

Vergil *Georgics* I in *Virgil* edited and translated by John Jackson (Oxford 1921)

Whallon, William *Formula, Character, and Context: Studies in Homeric, Old English, and Old Testament Poetry* (Cambridge, Mass, Harvard University Press 1969)

Whallon, William, and others 'Allegory, Tropology, or Neither' *Anglo-Saxon England* 2 (1973) 285–302

Whitelock, Dorothy *The Beginnings of English Society* (Harmondsworth 1956)

William of Malmesbury *Gesta pontificum anglorum* edited by N.E.S.A. Hamilton in *Chronicles and Memorials of Great Britain and Ireland during the Middle Ages* (London 1870)

Williams, David 'The Exile as Uncreator' *Mosaic* 8, 3 (1975) 1–14

Index